Acceptance *Is* Enough

If you've committed acts of homosexuality, you too can still be saved, because Christ said he will save *anyone* who comes unto him and believes upon him. What the law of the Old Testament could not do, in that it was weak through the flesh, God sending his own son in the likeness of sinful flesh, and *for* sin, condemned sin in the flesh. So no matter what the sin may be, the *person* can be saved if he or she comes to Christ because he became sin (all sin) for us. All sin is covered by His atoning blood... *from page 124.*

AS STRAIGHT AS AN ARROW

Exposing the Modern Myths of Homosexuality

by
Stanton P. McCoy

Published by DC Publishing
P.O. Box 15115
Youngstown, OH 44515

Scripture quotations not otherwise identified are from the Authorized King James Version of the Bible.

Profound quotes from Founding Fathers, Presidents, Statesmen, and Scientists are from *America's God and Country Encyclopedia of Quotations.*

Library of Congress Catalog Card Number: 98-72302

ISBN 0-9644644-1-1

PRINTED IN THE UNITED STATES OF AMERICA

Dedication

This writing is dedicated to those men and women who are now, more than ever, becoming active behind their faith, and as a result, are restoring the traditional moral values that once made our country deserve the admirable title of "One nation under God."

CONTENTS

May the words written herein glorify God,

who is the Author of the writer.

INTRODUCTION

"In the beginning God created the heaven and the earth."
"The grace of our Lord Jesus Christ be with you all. Amen."

These are the First and the Last statements of the HOLY BIBLE. They tell us a lot about what the best selling book of all time has to say to us. Many people today, especially regular church members, are familiar with these two statements. They are also familiar with many of the stories in this "Book of books." The overwhelming majority of people today, however, cannot come remotely close to naming all sixty-six books that make up the Bible. Yet it is *this* book that contains the most important and profound information *ever* written!

The Holy Bible is self-pronounced. That means that it clearly stands on its own authority. It is the inspired and infallible word of God written to man—for man's own sake! It tells us where we came from, what our purpose for being here is, and where we are going. It contains the real secrets to success, the answers to our questions. If read in humility of heart, its significance is understood in our lives, here and now, today. With all this vital information at our fingertips, we may be inclined to ask *what could be more important?*

As we search the sacred writings of the Old and New Testaments that make up the Holy Bible, we find that they describe a code of conduct that, if followed, makes for prosperous living. They also describe what happens to those who do not live by this code. And, within this code of conduct, the Holy Scriptures declare that homosexuality is *wrong.*

In response to the recent push by the media and other certain groups to declare otherwise, this book has been written. It has been written as a call to repentance to those who are living the gay lifestyle. It has also been written as a wake up call to the true Church to inform the members therein of the escalation of the gay rights movement occurring in America today, and of the implications that movement can have upon our society as a whole.

Before we begin, let me emphatically state that no one living today can completely comprehend the full glory of God's holiness or his perfect righteousness because the minds of men have been clouded by sin. However, the sharp decline in the spiritual state of our society can be readily seen when we compare the holy and righteous lifestyles of our Lord, Jesus Christ and his earthly mother, Mary, with the sharp contrasting lifestyles of the man and woman today who are living the gay lifestyle. A nearly unthinkable comparison, and yet perhaps a necessary one in order that *all* may see that when light is shed upon darkness, when holiness exposes its direct opposite—*sin*, then the ugliness of that sin is revealed.

Through the pages that follow, the author shall fire an arrow that will penetrate the hearts of those who are willing to listen to reason. In some, the arrow will have a positive if not profound effect in their lives, as they bear witness to the truth of this extremely important subject. In others, however, it will undoubtedly act as a weapon that will stir up dissension. In either case, the arrow shall have hit its target, for the arrow represents unwavering truth—truth that cannot and *will not* be swayed by the opinions of man. The arrow separates truth from error. The arrow *is* Jesus Christ.

Indeed, God *did* create the heaven and the earth. He also created the human race. And, He has offered us pardon for our sins if we repent and accept Christ. With this writing, it is the author's hope that the reader will be able to at least catch a glimpse of the holiness and perfect righteousness that God illuminates and wills to impart to his people. In doing so, may we gain a better understanding of the need for a new level of faith we as a nation need to embrace, and subsequently act upon. With this in mind, let us turn our attention to the ensuing chapters...

Chapter One

A DEGENERATE SOCIETY

The Result

*God has given them over to shameful passions.
Even the women pervert the natural use of their
sex by unnatural acts. In the same way, the men
give up natural sexual relations with women and
burn with passion for each other.*

ON APRIL 30, 1997, AMERICA WITNESSED A SHARP
decline in the moral fabric of our nation. The Society that once
so proudly and unashamedly declared "In God We Trust!" stood
by and watched a day of infamy for the character of the nation as
several television programs promoted the acceptance of
homosexuality. One program in particular, the sitcom *Ellen,* was
the coup de grace of the escalating gay rights movement of the
past decade.

On that program, the main character, Ellen Morgan
(portrayed by real life pro-gay activist Ellen DeGeneres) decided
to publicly announce to her friends that she was "gay." The
entire show revolved around Ellen's struggle to tell her friends,
and how she finally decided to invite them over for a party where
her sole purpose was to tell them what her sexual preference was!

The promoters of the program called it a "Coming out of the closet party." The advertisements that led up to the program called it "*The* Episode." Famed talk show hostess, Oprah Winfrey, played the role of Ellen's therapist on the program. During one of their sessions together, Ellen admitted that she preferred women over men. The "therapist" (who is African American) not only consoled her and condoned her behavior, but also went as far as to make comparisons to the intolerance shown toward blacks (several decades ago) to the intolerance shown today toward those members of society who come forth and publicly declare that they are living the gay lifestyle.

Earlier, on the same day that the Ellen program had aired, the *Oprah* talk show staged an hour long sit down with guest Ellen DeGeneres. That program promoted the acceptance of the gay lifestyle as well. DeGeneres' live-in girlfriend, Anne Heche was also invited on the Oprah Winfrey talk show that day. During the program, Ellen said she believed that she was born gay, but her girlfriend, Heche openly admitted to having "turned gay" only after having met Ellen. Heche said prior to Ellen, she had strictly "heterosexual affairs." This confounded hostess, Oprah, who had obviously bought lock-stock-and-barrel the lie of genetic homosexuality. "Now I'm confused." said Oprah, and she then told her guests to continue, she wanted to know more. So Ellen said (in such a manner as to gain sympathy from the viewing audience) that all she wanted to be was like "anyone else." She said she wants to have a partner for life, a home, and possibly children someday.

Although Ellen admitted that Heche was not her *first* lover, she unashamedly declared that they were now "soul mates." She also said she frequently has given thanks to God for having sent her someone like Heche. During the program, both DeGeneres and her girlfriend went on to say that all they want to do is "to live the truth." They said this *several* times.

Is Ellen DeGeneres, like Oprah Winfrey, confused? Is she a very confused and deceived individual, or a very sly one? If she is the ladder, she may have been mocking God for speaking about "living the truth" for the only real truth is found in Jesus

Christ, who said "Go and sin no more." This is not an unreasonable conclusion to reach, for a few years back DeGeneres made her living as a stand-up comedian whom pretended to have humorous conversations with God over the telephone.

Is Homosexuality Biblically Wrong?

During the Oprah program, a man in the audience challenged Ellen's gay lifestyle as being wrong—*biblically* wrong. Ellen's response was that her lifestyle is "not a choice" but rather it is "who she is." After the man had expressed that he did not dislike Ellen as a person, but that it was her lifestyle that is in error, another man in the audience stood up, and after stating that he was a Christian, went on to rebuke the first man's response by saying "The Bible also goes a step further and says "He who is without sin cast the first stone!" Although no one was throwing stones at Ellen DeGeneres that day, but merely trying to point out what God's word has to say on the subject, the audience sided with the second man, and with Ellen DeGeneres and *her way* of life.

This comes as no surprise. The world has always sided with that which chases after the lusts of the flesh over that which holds on to the respect and dignity of the spirit. Ever since the fall of Eve in the Garden of Eden, and then her enticement of Adam to do the same, the world has walked according to its weaknesses. But even so, we need to be very clear regarding this matter, for the *Bible* is very clear. Make no mistake, for God is serious when it comes to sexual impurity. He condemns the unnatural acts of gay sex.

Christian Rebukes Christianity?

If the first man, who had told Ellen that her lifestyle was that of sin, would have thought about it quickly enough, he could have responded to the "Christian" man's rebuttal with these words: "Yes, Christ did say "He who is without sin, let him cast the first stone." But he also said, in the same incident, "*...go and sin no more.*" {See John 8:11}.

To those who actually read the Bible, it was clear that most of the audience were not aware that the so-called self-professed "Christian" had taken one verse of scripture and used it *out of context* to fit his own viewpoint. As with any book, proper terminology is defined by context (what the chapter is all about). The surrounding passages tell us what certain individual verses are saying. In other words, the part of a statement that precedes or follows a word or passage influencing its meaning *is* context. So to put the verse that the "Christian" man used into perspective, all one needs to do is to put it back into context by turning to it in the Bible. *There* we find that the whole incident in which these words were spoken took place when some scribes and Pharisees brought a woman who had been caught in the very act of adultery into the presence of Jesus. The incited crowd said that in the law that Moses had commanded them, such a woman should be stoned, and they asked Jesus "What sayoust thou?" Then Jesus, as though he did not hear them, bent down and wrote something on the ground. So they continued to press him for an answer. Then Jesus stood and said, "He that is without sin among you, let him first cast a stone at her." {John 8:7}. And then he stooped down again and continued to write something on the ground.

Perhaps what each of the scribes and Pharisees saw there written on the ground by the finger of Jesus that day was their own *personal* worst sins. With all the other miracles that Jesus performed, this does not seem like an unreasonable conclusion to reach. In any case, the Bible does not tell us this, but it does tell us that being convicted by their own conscience, that they each went out one by one without casting any stones at the woman. They all left until the only two left there were the woman and Jesus. Then Jesus raised himself up and asked her "Woman, where are your accusers? Hath no man condemned thee?" The woman looked around, saw no one, and realized that she had just been saved. And then she replied "No man, Lord." And Jesus said "Neither do I condemn thee: *go and sin no more.*" {John 8:10-11}. (Emphasis added).

Now if you will notice the words that have been emphasized here, you will see that here was a woman who had done a terrible thing. She had abandoned the trust of her husband by having sex with another man—a sin punishable by death! (God is serious about sexual sin). Because it was one of the customary laws of the land, this woman had to have known that if she were ever caught having sexual relations with another man, she would be stoned to death. Yet she still let her desire for the lust of the flesh overpower her reasoning faculty. *And she got caught!* She would have been stoned had it not been for Jesus saving her. Yes, she was saved that day, but she was also warned to "go and sin no more." So what the second man said that day on the Oprah show (which the audience applauded) was, in effect, the condoning of sin by using words of Scripture out of context, whereas the truth regarding the matter is that Jesus was *condemning* sexual immorality, not *condoning* it.

Media Still Not Finished

After the *Oprah* and the *Ellen* shows had aired that day, the media wasn't finished yet. *Prime Time Live* also aired a program later that night that promoted the acceptance of the gay lifestyle. They interviewed the parents of Ellen DeGeneres. Although they were at first shocked by their daughter's real life confession, her parents finally came to accept their daughter's lifestyle. "She is a good girl." Her mother said. Her father took a little longer to "come around" but he too is now confused.

On the surface many people may see Ellen DeGeneres as a decent person; a comedian who just so happened to have fallen in love with a woman instead of a man. But upon a closer look, the facts reveal that her lifestyle has not been a pretty one. She has engaged in immoral, unhealthy, and unnatural sexual behavior, has mislead countless others into believing that it's "okay to be gay," that it's not a choice, but "who you are," and has gotten up on stage and made jokes about the Sovereign Lord of the Universe!

On the day of April 30, 1997, not only had the TV media aired three programs that diligently promoted the acceptance of the gay lifestyle, but the local news stations jumped on the pro-gay bandwagon as well. With one-sided interviews with the gay communities, the local news reporters managed to include a "fitting end" to a day of promoting the unconditional acceptance of the gay lifestyle across our nation.

Not A Religious Matter?

A week after the *Oprah* and *Ellen* shows had aired, due to all the feedback she got, Oprah Winfrey once again aired yet another program that centered on this highly controversial subject. She began by opening her talk show program with the announcement that "It was not going to be a religious discussion."

The panel of the show was stacked with a majority of guests who were obviously "pro-gay." There was a pro-gay psychologist. There was a pro-gay writer. The writer went as far as to say that the number of people born with so-called "homosexual genetic makeup" is greater than those who are born left-handed! Other statements were made on the program such as "We should re-define and look at things (as a society) quite differently." (In other words, accept gay sex as normal behavior.) And "Each individual *evolves* in their sexuality." (In other words, over time we change our sexual preferences, and therefore change our sexual partners as well, and let words like love, honor, cherish, and commitment have altogether no meaning in our lives whatsoever.) These kind of statements went on and on, and about half way through the program Oprah herself said "Open your minds...a little further..."

One thing for sure on the program was that most of the guests were confused. Perhaps the program should have carried the title "Dazed and Confused." There was one man there however who may have seen through all the hype, for he said something that silenced them all. What he said was, in effect, if homosexuality is okay, then "Why is it bad to teach this to our children?" When he made *that* statement, you could have heard a pin drop. No one had an answer to his question. Not the pro-gay guests. Not the psychologist who was trying to rationalize sexual perversion with normalcy. Not the writer who believed that homosexuality is of genetic origin. No, not even Oprah Winfrey had an answer for this. Just silence.

Other Pro-Homosexual Programs

If you missed the Ellen show, the two Oprah shows, or Prime Time Live, perhaps you have caught one of the other recent prominent TV shows that have been promoting the gay lifestyle. *Dawson's Creek*, for example introduced the first openly gay teen to hit a television series, and the comedy series' *Will & Grace* and *Spin City* both have gay characters represented. At the time of this writing, an animated program entitled *The Sissy Duckling* was scheduled to air on HBO (September, 1999). The so-called "animated update" of Han's Christian Anderson's *The Ugly Duckling* tells the story of Elmer, a "unique" little duckling who doesn't quite fit in with the rest of the flock.

Some programs were pushing the gay agenda even before the Ellen "coming out" program had aired. Around a week before the *The* Ellen episode had aired, the sitcom *Susan* had already aired an episode that depicted one of the regular stars of that show eagerly awaiting to reunite with his brother—but the reunion turned sour after he found out that his brother had chosen to live the gay lifestyle. Being a womanizer, the regular character had a hard time with his brother's confession, and at first he rejected him, and then tried to avoid him. But by the end of the show, the constant prodding of the rest of the characters had persuaded him to accept his brother's choice of the gay lifestyle.

Other recognizable programs that had preceded *Ellen* include the hit comedy series *Roseanne*, which in 1994 featured a "romantic kiss" between two women. The show *Relativity* also showed woman "lovers" kissing, and in 1996 the sitcom *Friends* aired a program in which two woman characters "got married" to each other.

What The Media Is Providing For America

What is our national media trying to tell us today? To "Go and sin no more?" Hardly. Instead, they are bombarding us with just the opposite message! Consider the Walt Disney Company for example. Once a well-trusted family oriented company, the Disney Company now has included a sex agenda in its entertainment empire, and parents should be leery when they hear words like "gay" uttered by the company because they may not be referring to children having a merry old time!

The Walt Disney Company is the parent company of the ABC television network that aired *Ellen*. As of June, 1999, the Disney Company had held its ninth annual celebration of "Gay Days" at its Disney World theme park in Orlando, Florida. Many of the "straight" visitors (who were given no prior warning that the theme park was catering to an onslaught of people exposing the gay lifestyle) have been shocked by gross displays of same-sex affection, and they have had to turn their children away from the scene.

But the Disney Company has not stopped there. It now also participates in gay and lesbian film and video festivals, advertises in gay magazines, publishes books on homosexuality for children such as *Growing Up Gay* (Through *Hyperion Press*), as well as books about transvestites. They have even produced pro-gay movies (through *Miramax* and *Hollywood Pictures*).

Because of the production of this type of material by the once trusted company, in 1997 the Southern Baptist Convention headed up a boycott of the Disney Company and all of its products. Other organizations such as the American Family Association, Assemblies of God, Focus On The Family, Free Will Baptists, Presbyterian Church of America, Citizens for a Better America, Concerned Women for America, and others have joined in on this boycott.

All we have to do to understand how media groups like Disney are reshaping our culture is to compare our religious freedoms, our lifestyles, and our language today to that of thirty years ago. Any night of the week you can turn on your TV and watch what just a handful of people in Hollywood have dreamed up to "entertain" and *teach* us. You can watch one of the many sitcoms and learn either how to be antagonistic toward one another or how to shed humor on sin.

If you are a moviegoer, you can glue your eyes to one of the many movies they provide us with today, and be "entertained" by all manner of violence and or sexual immorality for an evening.

Perhaps you're either a homebody or a young child, and you have time to take in a talk show during the day. What will that provide you with? Ninety percent of the time (or more) they will provide you with some people that they have dug up that have real nasty problems, and who are willing and eager to show you those nasty problems.

If you find that you are a real couch potato and enjoy watching soap operas all day, you can store up regularly broadcast acts of adultery, hatred, lying, cheating, back-stabbing, and plain old evil into your subconscious mind from nearly each and every episode. It's all in a day's work for the producers of those programs.

If you enjoy slander and seeing other people's pain, you can tune in to one of the tabloid news shows such as *Inside Edition* or *Hard Copy* where you can catch up on all the juicy gossip of the day. One scandal after another there.

The media doesn't want you to forget what's "going on out there" for any lengthy period of time. So if you actually turn off the tube and go to the store to get groceries or something, they will catch up with you there too. The checkout lines are stacked full of magazines and tabloids with pictures of half-naked people and headlines of "the latest."

If you will step back and take a logical look at what the media is providing—in view of the Big Picture—you will see that they are, in effect, promoting *hatred, envy, strife,* and *sexual immorality.* That's what they're providing us with, but they don't want to appear totally negative, so they will throw in a good story ever so often. That is how they gain credibility with their audiences.

Why? MONEY. Their reasoning is that "No news is good news." If the subject matter isn't shocking, it doesn't turn heads. According to them, if it doesn't turn heads, it doesn't turn dollars. This "excuse" simply doesn't wash because family friendly and wholesome shows usually get better ratings than do shows portraying violence and or smut. Surveys even show that the American public is *concerned* with sexual immorality and the portrayal of the gay lifestyle on TV and at the movies. Nevertheless, the gay agenda for prime time viewing on TV has exploded in recent years. In 1992, *Entertainment Weekly* named the Gay & Lesbian Alliance Against Defamation (GLAAD) as one of Hollywood's most powerful entities. This group has not only reached Hollywood insiders, but it has also impacted the mass media through magazines, newspapers, and other visibility campaign efforts, and the *Los Angeles Times* has described them as one of the most successful organizations lobbying the media for inclusion. On its website, GLAAD boasts about the number of lesbian, gay, or transgender characters that are scheduled in the primetime TV Lineup for the 1999-2000 season (28 in all) and yet they also complain that the number is too low! And so they continue to lobby the TV networks for more "gay characters," more "gay representations," and more "romantic encounters" between gay characters. Despite the fact that all the above is occurring, many of the media spin doctors and gay activists are saying that there is no gay agenda occurring in America today!

The bottom line is this: America is having an agenda pushed upon it. And those who are pushing that agenda are pushing for a society that fully accepts gay sex as a normal sexual behavior. In doing so, they are trying to re-label perversion as an "alternative lifestyle." As Herb Holliger, press spokesman for the Southern Baptist Convention put it "Someone is pushing an agenda—and that's to make homosexuality a normal part of American culture...They're determined to depict their lifestyle as a normal one. Well, it isn't. It's far from normal."

An Attempt To Glorify Sin

The rainbow flag that an artist created in response to a San Francisco gay activist's call for "a need for a community symbol" represents the gay rights movement. The pro-gay activists say it represents diversity. Those who are promoting the gay rights agenda have been trying to expound the message that "gays" are a race—a minority race—that is. But in reality, are they not just people from all walks of life who have chosen to engage in sexual acts with members of the same sex? Therefore, would it not be a similar attempt to justify or glorify the acts of pedophilia if the individuals who are engaging in *that* type of sin were to create a flag of their own as well? After all, aren't pedophiles a minority too? Isn't it closer to the truth to say that the promotion of the gay lifestyle is just an attempt to glorify sin?

Now let us turn our attention back to the first man on the infamous Oprah show, which aired on April 30. I'm sure that the man knew many passages of Scripture, for at one point he tried to point out to Ellen and her girlfriend that they are trying to glorify sin (at which the audience hissed and booed). Under the pressure of that audience, who had obviously sided with Ellen DeGeneres and the so-called "Christian" man in the audience, this first man probably could not bring to mind some of the verses of the Bible that condemn the sin of same sex perversion. Perhaps part of what he did actually say was edited out.

So that *you* may know what the Bible and its Author have to say about this controversial subject, this book, unlike parts of those programs, will not be cut short. Throughout the following pages you will learn the truth about what the Holy Scriptures call an "abomination." You will learn the hard truth about the end result of God's judgment upon this sin. But you will also learn a lot about *hope*. You will see that God is not only a god of justice, but is a god of love and enduring mercy as well. And hopefully, some of you who are as lost sheep who have been *deceived* by the media (and others) will be found, and will be persuaded to come back and claim your inheritance into the Kingdom that God has been preparing for those who trust upon Him. By being patient, and by reading on, you will soon discover the truth, and then hopefully will make a decision to reject that which has been nothing other than a *choice*.

What's On The Agenda?

I have heard conversations between heterosexuals (straight people) who don't know much about what is contained in the Bible regarding homosexuality. I have heard them make statements such as "There is nothing wrong with it," "To each his own," and "What they do behind closed doors is their own business." Well if statements such as this are true, then let me paint a picture for you of what our society will become like if the items on the pro-gay activists' agenda come to fruition.

Unholy Matrimony

In December of 1997 a Gallup Poll revealed that 68% of Americans oppose homosexual marriage. Nevertheless, there is an ugly monster on the horizon, and it's called legalized same-sex marriage. First and foremost, political activists who are fighting for gay rights want to see the day when couples who are living the gay lifestyle can get legally married in this country. As the Human Rights Campaign (HRC), the nation's largest gay and lesbian political organization has stated "…we will continue with every ounce of energy, commitment and vigor to achieve our dream of complete equality, including full and equal civil marriage rights."

If organizations such as this get their way, it would restructure the traditional family of our society almost overnight. To live together under law and receive the same benefits that heterosexual married couples receive means that same-sex married couples would begin to enjoy the following:

<u>Rights</u> <u>To</u> <u>Living</u> <u>Quarters</u>: *Landlords* would be required by law to accept them as tenants.

<u>Job</u> <u>Discrimination</u> <u>Protection</u>: *Employers* would not be allowed to discriminate against them when deciding whether or not to hire them for jobs. This means that those living the gay lifestyle could be employed by your local Christian bookstore! As with Black and Hispanic minorities, a certain percentage of them would actually be required by law to be hired.

<u>Job</u> <u>Benefits</u>: *Employers* would be required by law to offer them all the same benefits that they do normal married couples.

<u>Insurance</u> <u>Benefits</u>: *Insurance companies* would be forced to change their policies to include them in the definition of that which constitutes "family" and provide them with the same types of benefits.

<u>Parental</u> <u>Rights</u>: *Adoption agencies* would be required to consider them without regards to their sexual preference as potential legal guardians or "parents" for children that are available for adoption. Then these "parents" would be able to teach their children that there "is no such thing as sexual perversion—that it's okay to be gay!"

<u>Educational</u> <u>Rights</u>: *Sex Education teachers* in public schools

would have to teach children that lasciviousness is an acceptable sexual behavior—that such behavior is merely an "alternative lifestyle."

<u>Spousal</u> <u>Benefits</u>: *Court Judges* would be forced to issue alimony and or child support injunctions against same-sex "mates" who break their vows and go astray. The courts would then have to define who is the "wife" or "mother" and who is the "husband" or "father" in all divorce cases as well as determine who would get possession of property and or custody of children.

<u>Defamation</u> <u>Protection</u>: *Writers, Publishers,* and *Preachers,* would be sued for libel for printing words that are defamatory towards those who are living in this sin—regardless of whether or not those words are true and or Biblical.

<u>Freedom</u> <u>Of</u> <u>Speech</u>: On the one side, *preachers, newspaper columnists, libraries, Christian radio and TV broadcasts,* and others would have their "opinions" censored out if those opinions speak out against homosexuality. They would be deemed "too controversial" by the liberal media and Big Brother, Inc. On the other side, *Libraries, Bookstores, Newspapers, Educators,* and others would be pressured to offer all manner of pro-gay literature to the general public.

Some of these things are already coming to pass, but as the saying goes, *We ain't seen nothing yet....*If the courts legalize homosexual marriages, *we will.*

Acceptance Not Enough

The rights and benefits mentioned here are not enough for the bold and more outspoken of the gay rights movement. There is a vain pride attached to the ego of some of the advocates of this sinful lifestyle. They are striving not only to achieve acceptance, and then let others live as they will. For them, that is not enough. Even the drastic cultural reform that will take place if same-sex marriage licenses are passed out is not enough. They want more! Not only do they want to push Godless values upon society at large (even though society does not want them) which, by definition, makes them *radicals,* they also want to pollute our society with downright atrocious demands. These are written statements that are already outlined in the gay rights agenda. They have entitled their document the *"Platform for Lesbian, Gay, and Bi Equal Rights and Liberation."* Within this document, among other outlandish goals are these:

* To lower the age of legal consent. (This would allow adults to legally have sex with minors).
* To force the insurance companies of America to actually pay for sex-change operations.
* To pressure the government into using tax dollars (*our* tax dollars) to pay for sterile needles for drug addicts.
* To sue preachers for hate crimes and bigotry.

If these goals are met, they will be nothing less than atrocities within our once great nation. And who will we have to blame for these abominable acts? Those impassioned goal-oriented and mission driven gay rights activists *and* the rest of us who sat on our hands and did absolutely nothing to prevent them from happening!

What's Already Happening

In our nation today, the gay rights movement has spread wide and far. Kenyon College in Gambier, Ohio, for example, is one of a growing number of colleges and universities nationwide that has adopted policies that allow the "domestic partners" of gay and lesbian faculty (and other employees) to access the same benefits, including health insurance coverage, that have traditionally been available only to the spouses of heterosexual employees. According to an article released in June, 1999, by the Human Rights Campaign, some ninety colleges and universities now have similar policies.

Cornell University has gotten in on the act too. They are just one of several universities that have now adopted sex gender study programs. Cornell even has a course called "The Sexual Child" which is being taught by an English professor who challenges the "belief" that pedophilia is bad.

Many other colleges and universities have also opened dorms for their "homosexual students." Boston College's "Gay

Community" for instance, even staged a drag show featuring one student dressed as a priest who fondled the male student's private parts!

The colleges and universities aren't the only ones who are bowing down to the demands of the powerful gay lobby groups. Corporate America has, as of late, been doing the same thing. In 1991 for example, the *Lotus Corporation* decided to extend health care benefits to its so-called "gay employees" and to their live-in partners. Since then, other major companies have followed suit, and now *American Express Financial Advisers, Apple Computer, AT&T, Eastman Kodak, EDS, Hewlett Packard, IBM, Merrill Lynch, Microsoft, Northern Telecom, Sun Microsystems* and others are offering these "domestic partner" benefits to their gay employees, while denying those same benefits to the live-in partners of their straight employees.

If you're flying these days, don't be too surprised to see two men holding hands beside you. *American Airlines* has officially listed "sexual orientation" as one of its employee non-discriminatory benefits. The company also offers benefits for gay couples through airfares and unashamedly calls itself the "Official Carrier" of a gay schoolteachers group! The airline has sponsored gay pride events and has given financial support to gay activist groups such as GLAAD. One such contribution was $50,000 to underwrite GLAAD's media awards. GLAAD nominated *Corpus Christi* as the year's "Outstanding New York Theatre Production." The play depicts a "gay Christ" who has sex with his disciples, and denounces "homophobia."

Not only are some of the colleges, universities, and businesses incorporating these types of benefits, but some of the governing authorities within some of our major cities are doing the same. Their behaviors are sounding like something taken straight out of the nineteenth chapter of Genesis. For example, in March 1996, the Mayor of San Francisco conducted a mass "wedding" of gay couples. That same year, San Francisco became the first city in our nation to execute an order (the Equal Benefits Ordinance) that requires that businesses contracting with the city must offer domestic partner benefits. In this same city, where gay activists march down the streets in what they call "gay pride parades" holding signs that read *"STOP THE HATE"* and *"INTOLERANCE"* some gay radicals sued a city pastor, made threats against his children, and then finally bombed his house! His crime? He wrote a book entitled *When The Wicked Seize A City.*

Other places are now sinking low as well. In Los Angeles for example, over 800 staff members of the City Attorney's office attended sensitivity training classes on "sexual orientation in the workplace." In the city of Provincetown, Massachusetts, school board officials have decided that the teaching of homosexual values—starting with preschool children—should be part of the "curriculum." The superintendent of the schools there said "We're going to be an agent for change." And in a city in New Jersey, two men were granted joint custody of a two-year-old boy through adoption, making *that* state the first in the country to allow gay or unmarried couples to jointly adopt.

There is a book out which bears a title that would be a fitting description of some of these cities today—it's called *Slouching Towards Gomorrah.*

On The Legal Front

The gay rights movement has taken the battle into the courtrooms across our nation as well. In the state of Hawaii, for instance, over *seventy* percent of the population of the state is opposed to the legislation of same-sex marriages. However, a handful of liberal government officials there have kept on trying to push this legislation, and overthrow the will of the people! Why? Because they are being pressured by gay activist groups with political clout. These groups (and the liberal judges that do not oppose them) are trying to restructure our culture in accordance to their own desires. Some of these groups (such as GLAAD and the Freedom To Marry Coalition) have even organized what they refer to as "National Freedom to Marry Day." They have sponsored events nationwide to fight for the "equal rights" of those men and women who are living the gay lifestyle to be able to legally marry members of their own sex.

If just one state such as Hawaii gets away with legalizing homosexual marriages, then under the Constitution's Full Faith and Credit Clause, the other states in the union may have to recognize the "union" under the law. This means that gay couples could fly there to get their marriage license and then when they return home to your state, you could be *forced by law* to honor their unholy matrimony. As you have seen, whether you are a landlord, employer, teacher, or "whatever," you will have to "respect" their rights as married couples just as you would any other married couple.

Other states in which the will of the moral majority has been thrown out by liberal judges who are siding with gay activists include Colorado, New Jersey, and Ohio.

A Day Of Infamy

If the Christian Community sits idly by and ignores the gay rights movement, then April 30, 1997, may be the day that will go down in history as the day the once beautiful America got the blemish on her face that eventually led to her complete disfigurement! Then perhaps those who promoted this radical reform of our culture will, in remembrance of their victory, look back and pin-point this day as the turning point of their successes. Perhaps they will persuade our voted-in leaders of government to declare that even speech written or spoken against their way of life as a "hate crime." After all, why not? They already have the backing of our president and vice-president. The president has dedicated an entire month as "gay pride month" and during a recent speech to Hollywood, vice-president Al Gore praised *Ellen* for "...forcing Americans to look at sexual orientation in a more open light."

If the two highest ranking government officials of our nation are right, then perhaps the gay community will coin the day that *Ellen* aired the "coming out" episode as "National Gay Acceptance Day" and they will demand that we *all* be *forced* to observe it as a national holiday. If they get their way regarding this matter, they will have accomplished the feat of turning more people away from God (especially future generations) than perhaps any other single movement has in the entire history of this nation.

A Nation Slipping Into Depravity

Advocates that have either chosen or are backing the gay lifestyle are indeed trying to radically reshape America without regards to the nation's rich Christian heritage. In the parades, on the TV, on the radio, in the classrooms, in the courthouses, and at every level of government, the advocates of gay rights are pressing toward *their* mark. If they succeed in getting the passage of legalized same-sex marriages in this country, then this small group of extremists that consists of the gay community in affiliation with Hollywood (and just a few key players in Washington), will have succeeded in the inbreeding of sexually deviate lifestyles throughout America, and their actions will be upheld *by law!* And then the spiritual, mental, and physical state of the nation will have descended into the ugliness and depravity of a profligate lifestyle.

Do *you* want *your* children brought up in a society like the one I've described here? Do you want to see a society that has role models such as teachers, coaches, speakers, athletes, and even preachers who engage in this unhealthy lifestyle be able to tell those who look up to them that it's okay to do the same? Do you personally want to live in a society where everyone is expected, even *forced* to view it as normal?

I know I don't, for that is nothing less than a degenerate society. As for me and my house...we will serve the Lord.

Chapter Two

A DECEIVED SOCIETY

The Cause

*For the time will come when they will not endure
sound doctrine; but after their own lusts shall they
heap to themselves teachers, having itching ears;
And they shall turn away from the truth, and shall
be turned unto fables.*

2 Timothy 4:3-4   Holy Bible

LET US SEPARATE TRUTH FROM ERROR. There are those who believe that the Bible is the infallible word of the living God. There are others who say they do not believe it. There are still others who say they believe the Bible, yet make no effort to read it, and therefore do not learn *of* God.

Those who believe *know* that *all* scripture is given by inspiration of God, and is profitable for doctrine, for reproof, for correction, and for instruction in righteousness. Those who *say* they don't believe the Bible should at least believe in God for what can be known about Him is plain to them, for God himself made it plain. Ever since God created the world, His eternal power and divine nature have been clearly seen; they are perceived in the things that He has made. So those who *claim* to be atheists have no excuse at all! We'll get into more detail on

31

this in a later chapter, but for now I am reminded of a conversation I had several years ago with a man who was, at the time, my employer. We were sitting in a restaurant and I had turned our conversation onto the subject of the Bible. To my utter astonishment, he declared that he believed that the Bible was just a bunch of stories written by men who probably even included writers such as Aristotle, Plato, and Socrates! He said it was written by men such as these just to teach lessons to people of their day. "We even learned that in college." he said. I could hardly believe my ears!

Once again, let's separate truth from error. Yes, there is a God; the Bible *proves* it! And *this* book proves that the Bible proves it! So for those who don't believe... read on. And as for those who say they believe, but make no effort to learn of God— they too have become easy prey for a world under the rule of Satan.

A Real Devil?

Satan? You mean a *real* devil? Yes, there is a real devil, just as there is a real God, and a real Jesus Christ. But the followers of Satan would like us to believe that the devil is, at most, just a symbol for evil, and at the least, just a laughable cartoon figure with horns, a cloven hoof, and a forked tail who carries a pitchfork around prodding his victims with it. To some, he is merely a myth, to others, simply a superstition. It should come as no surprise that the world tries to downplay Satan's character and discredit him for his role against God and humanity, for the world also tries to discredit the Bible itself. Why? Because the scriptures offend most people by pointing out that human beings are no-good sinners who deserve eternal punishment in hell!

The Old Testament Devil

The Holy Scriptures paint a very different, a very *real* picture of the devil. This "enemy of everlasting life" is mentioned many times throughout the Bible, but not as a horny fork-tailed creature dwelling in a dimly lit underworld of some sort, but to the contrary, as an angel of light! {2Corinthians 11:14}. He is mentioned at the beginning of the Holy Bible as the one who took on the form of a serpent so he could *deceive* the first parents of the human family. {Genesis 3:1-5,13, 2Corinthians 11:3, Revelation 12:9, 20:2}.

In the Old Testament book of Job, we read how Satan approached God and God asked him if he had noticed the faithful servant, Job. Satan then challenged God by declaring that the only reason Job served God was because God had protected him and gave him plenty. {Job 1:6-12}. So in order to prove Job's faithfulness, God allowed Satan to take away all of Job's earthly possessions, including his family, but Job's integrity remained intact. So once again Satan approached God and declared that "All that a man has, he will give for his own life." And Satan tempted God to smite Job's flesh and bones and as a result, Job would, according to Satan, curse God to his face. But God did not lay his hand upon Job, instead he *allowed* Satan to smite Job's flesh. {Job 2:1-7}. So Satan put sore boils on Job's flesh from head to toe. So sore were the boils, that Job used a piece of broken pottery to scrape his sores. At that point, Job's own wife told him he should curse God and die. Even "religious friends" came to visit Job, and they tried to convince him that he was a terrible sinner to have deserved such a punishment from God, and they tried to convince him to repent. Despite all of his afflictions and the stress from his wife and "friends," Job did not curse God. God then blessed him even more than he had originally.

The Old Testament also mentions Satan, the accuser, in a vision given to the prophet Zechariah that shows how Satan was trying to bring accusation against the high priest, Joshua, while standing in the presence of the angel of the Lord. But the angel rebuked Satan saying that Joshua was like a stick that was snatched from the fire. {Zechariah 3:1-2}.

The Origin Of Satan

Satan (which literally means adversary or opposer) was *not* created by God! But a beautiful angel who was very intelligent and very high in rank named Lucifer was created by God. {Isaiah

14:12-15}. This angel, probably the most attractive of all the many angels of God, was so majestic in his creation that he was even called "Son of the morning." He was the "anointed cherub" who presided on the holy mountain of God, and even walked in the midst of the stones of fire. He was perfect in all ways until he became vane in his imagination and corrupted his wisdom by reason of his brightness. He even began to covet the very position of God himself! He stirred up dissension in heaven among other angels, and a third of them joined him in rebellion against God. In the sixty-sixth and final book of the Bible, the Revelation, it mentions a war in heaven between Michael and his angels and Satan and his followers, wherein Satan's demonic army looses and are all cast out of heaven and down to the earth. It goes on to say "Therefore rejoice ye heavens and ye that dwell in them. But woe to the inhabitants of the earth and of the sea for the devil is come down to you, having great wrath, for he hath but a short time." {Revelation 12:7-12}.

The Roaring Lion

Jesus knows that there is a real devil. Through men, Satan tried to have Jesus murdered when he was but an infant. He also tried to tempt Jesus to sin at various times throughout his earthly ministry. {Mark 1:13}. During his ministry, Jesus warned both his followers *and* his enemies about Satan. Near the end of Jesus' ministry, Satan entered into the apostle Judas Iscariot so that he would betray Jesus and turn him over to the chief priests and scribes who were planning to kill him. After Jesus had been put to death on the cross, rose again the third day, taught his disciples for forty days, then ascended into heaven, the *apostles* began to warn *society* about Satan. The leading apostle, Peter, told other followers of Christ to "Be sober, be vigilant, because your adversary the devil, as a roaring lion, roams about, seeking whom he may devour." {1 Peter 5:8}.

Called By Any Other Name

Throughout the pages of the Bible and other records of antiquity, this angelic-being-gone-sour has been called by many names. He has been known as "an angel of light," "the accuser," "the tempter," "the wicked one," "the evil one," "that serpent of old," "Father of the lie," "murderer from the beginning," "the prince of the power of the air," "the prince of darkness," "the great dragon," and "the god of *this* world" just to name a few. But out of all the titles given him, I think the one that the human race needs to be aware of most is "Master of Deception."

Yes, Satan the devil is real. He is very real indeed, and he is very good at what he likes to do best: *deceive*. He is Commander and Chief over one third of the (fallen) hosts of heaven, and along with them he exerts power not only over individuals, but over whole nations, and even the entire world!

Satan's Tools Of The Trade: People, Propaganda, and Pride

When Satan exerts his power, he influences *people*. Most of his influence over people is derived from his ability to deceive them. He has sown the seeds of doubt into the minds of everyone since the very beginning. "Yea, hath God said, Ye shall not eat of every tree of the garden?" And when the woman replied and said that God had commanded them not to eat of the tree of the knowledge of good and evil for in the day that they did they would surely die, Satan declared "Ye shall not surely die!" But in the very day that they ate the forbidden fruit, sin entered the world, and the parents of the human race died *spiritually*. This for the fact that they disobeyed God, and therefore separated themselves from Him. They also began to die *physically*, and they died *in the day* that they ate thereof, because one day is with the Lord as a thousand years, and a thousand years as one day. {See 2Peter 3:8}. Adam lived nine hundred thirty years, and then he died. And so the first parents of the human family gave up an eternity of health and happiness for a few moments (in comparison) of what they perceived as pleasure. They were deceived.

We Didn't Start The Fire

The song by Billy Joel which has the lyrics "We didn't start the fire, it was always burning since the world's been turning..." contains some truth to it. No, we didn't start the fire—Satan did! But we did take off our clothes (of righteousness) and jump right into the fire...and we've been getting burnt ever since!

Yes Satan uses people to do his bidding, and it is through *some* people that Satan manipulates *many* people. He does this through the uses of propaganda and pride. As a result, we now live in a society in which a mere fraction of the people are suppressing and twisting truth to make sin appear to be widely accepted. As we have seen, they are doing this with the aid of the government, the courts, the entertainment and national news media, and even some of the public schools! What it boils down to is that they are using propaganda, and because of their pride and their desire to go unopposed, they are using censorship to achieve their desired goals. The end result is that the *majority* of people in America today are being deceived, and our nation as a whole is quickly becoming one that tolerates sin but does not tolerate anger towards sin.

Evolutionists: They Pulled The Bible Out By The Roots...

Over all of our recorded history Satan has spun lies to beguile certain people into doubting God and his word. One of them is the lie of evolution. Evolution should adequately be renamed to express more clearly what it really stands for: *Evil*ution. "Yea, hath *man* said that there *really is* a God?" sputters the serpent. And thus he convinces a few people that man is his own "god" and that he was not created at all, but just came strolling into being by happenstance. "And oh what a good tale this is to weave...muses the devil...for if they believe this one, then Christ's mission becomes purposeless, and the entire Christian religion becomes a farce!"

Yes, Satan is hard at work today undermining the beliefs of even the "elect" of God. He has undermined many people by using the "more learned" of our society to expound a view of human origins that diametrically opposes the Genesis account of creation, because he knows that Genesis is not only the foundational book of God's Holy Word, but it is the foundational structure of Christianity itself. Simply stated, evolution undermines Christianity. It turns people away from their faith in their Creator, and it turns them "unto a fable."

...By Telling A Tall Tale

Even the tale itself that Satan has told men such as Charles Darwin (the English naturalist who became the father of the evolutionary movement) and that famed American astronomer, Carl Sagan, seems to be constantly *evolving*. Satan, having been around a lot longer than man, knows that we were not present during the formation of the universe, so he whispers into the itching ears of these men like Darwin (who are eager to declare their "findings" to their fellow man) and says "Where were *you* in the beginning?" And then the Master of Deception goes to work and begins to weave a fantastic tale...

"Have you not heard, have you not understood that *in the beginning* trillions of particles of physical matter were scattered throughout the universe as the result of an explosion of inconceivable proportions? Do you not realize that the explosion was the result of compressed hydrogen matter? It was a "Big Bang" that sent dust, gas, and radiation (cosmic debris) hurling out across all that there *wasn't* to form the basis for all that there *is*. When some of the particles of debris finally stopped dancing across space, and each cluster found its own resting place, gravity took charge and pulled the particles inward together to form those great balls of fire that you call "stars."

"Over time, more space debris slowed down and eventually stopped around those stars, forming planets. Ah yes, and around your star, nine such planets formed, along with other space rocks such as meteoroids, asteroids, comets, and the thirty-one moons that now comprise the make up of your solar system. Which brings us down here to the little planet that you call "earth."

"Were you aware that the earth was formed around four and a half *billion* years ago? At the time of its formation until around 3.8 billion years ago, space debris bombarded the planet, leaving it uninhabitable. After the asteroid showers had ceased, and the boiling oceans cooled, somehow, just by chance, a group of subatomic particles began to coalesce into atoms. Over time, those atoms became molecules which formed into protein chains that became *cells*."

"The cells then began to form into plankton, bacteria, and algae which existed in the waters of the earth. These little organisms dominated the planet until a mere five hundred and fifty million years ago! Then nature produced a biological "big bang" as well. Somehow, nobody knows just how, nature began to evolve its multi-celled algae into weird little creatures that crawled around on the ocean floors. Creatures that formed the foundational basis of almost all of your major branches of zoology began to emerge. Among the frenzy of organic life activity arose scores of bristle worms, mollusks, jellyfish, and sea cucumbers. And shortly thereafter, there arose a small creature with a flexible, but sturdy spinal rod. This strange little creature began to slither around in the ocean and became the progenitor of the chordate line; the oldest ancestor of the vertebrate branch of the animal kingdom! And thus life on earth had arrived!"

"The chordate eventually evolved into a fish that eventually evolved into an amphibian. The amphibian then later evolved into a reptile that crawled out of the primordial seas and while dragging itself through the mud, learned to breathe the air in order to adapt to its new environment. Since it needed a mate but was all alone, nature endowed it with multi-sex capabilities. It therefore reproduced itself. Then, along with its family, it pulled itself up over a hill and eventually evolved into an ape-like mammal so it could once again adapt to its new environment."

"It moved on from there into the caves where, over the years, adapted more and more to its environment, but only the fittest of these hump-backed mammals survived. With the passing of time, their bones began to straighten, they began to walk upright, and they learned how to shave. Those that survived, eventually began to learn *systematically*."

"Eventually, they became what you *are* today, and the rest, as they say... is history."

So there you have it. The way the human race came to be.

WRONG.

History Is *His* Story

Throughout human history, Satan has indeed played a tragic role in the affairs of men. But now, once again, let's separate truth from error. The story of how everything came from nothing; how beauty, order, and design all arrived by chance and out of chaos is a *lie.* It is a lie of the highest order, a fairy-tale concocted by Satan to deceive people.

Now for the truth: *This beautiful planet was brought to us through the courtesy of Almighty God!* This is not just a belief or an opinion on the part of the author; it is a *fact.* It's a better song to sing, a better tale to tell, and it is based on facts, not on inconclusive evidence, wishful thinking, fantasy, or fabrications of the truth (which are all found in the case of evolutionary theory). No, this is by far more, for it is factual, it is history, and it is based on *common sense.* It has purpose, meaning, and direction for life. The theory of evolution has none of these to offer. Creation is diametrically opposed to evolution because it is *the truth.*

True Science Speaks Out

According to the definition of science itself, evolution is not scientific and should not even be called a theory or even a hypothesis because it violates both the First and Second Laws of Thermodynamics. Evolution is none of these things, it is simply a *belief.* But it is a belief that has grown into a religion; an atheistic religion. Many so-called "scientists" today have let fabrications slip into a once highly integral field of study. With the aid of the media, they have claimed their "findings" to be "facts" when in truth, they are nothing of the sort. The whole sequence goes something like this:

1. A small piece of "evidence" is found that supposedly supports evolution.
2. The scientist forms a personal belief regarding the finding; begins to speculate.
3. The scientist's imagination of something grandeur in history begins to emerge.
4. The possibility of notoriety sets in.

5. A story about the finding is created with all the "trimmings."
6. The story is grandiloquently released to the media.
7. The media "puffs up" the story even more...

until what you end up getting are so-called "facts" about something that took place in history that have been all blown out of proportion. Most of the time what the average citizen ends up hearing on the radio, reading about in the paper, or seeing on TV is not true science at all, but rather *science fiction!*

Let's separate truth from error. The Scriptures give us the richest vestige of our human history that can be found *anywhere*, and yet they are ignored by many in the scientific community. The great deluge mentioned in the Bible, for example, that overwhelmed and inundated the entire planet leaving behind clear evidence in the rock formations of the rapid burial of all manner of life forms in abundance, is completely discarded by many geologists today. Nevertheless, since the publication of a book entitled *The Genesis Flood* in 1961, by hydraulic engineer Henry M. Morris and biblical scholar John C. Whitcomb, Jr., Creation Science has been opening the eyes of many a scientist.

In catastrophism (the study of what happens to earth materials when catastrophes occur), we often find clear evidence which refutes evolution. Since true science is the study of a body of facts systematically arranged to show the operation of general laws, the catastrophe of the eruption of Mount Saint Helens, on May 18, 1980, for example, forced many scientists to abandon their belief in the accuracy of the methods they had been accustomed to using for dating the ages of earth materials.

Evolution Devalues Human Life

Satan's goal or purpose seems to be to get all of mankind to turn away from their Creator. And how is Satan attempting to accomplish this great task? By forcing people to worship him instead? No. Even *he* knows that the angels and mankind have been created with one Supreme Prerogative: *the power of choice.* Satan knows that not all men will bow the knee to a tyrant, even if it will mean certain death if they don't. So instead, his methods are sly and cunning. His plan involves getting people to do what is wrong by making what they do appear to be beneficial, pleasant, pleasurable, innocent enough, or even justifiable. By doing this, he tries to get people to turn their backs on their one and only Creator. The Master of Deception even gets people to question God's very existence. Atheistic evolutionary teaching plants the seeds of doubt, which grow into the weeds of dissension. Then, when the question is raised "What is the purpose of life?" Satan whispers in our ears *"It is purposeless. Live for the pleasures of today, for there may be no tomorrow."* This is the same lie that Satan got men the likes of Marx, Lenin, Stalin, and Hitler to embrace. Their evolutionary thinking removed God from their societies and resulted in the communistic "Evil Empire" and the holocaust of Nazi Germany. Their rationale was "survival of the fittest." When we look up Darwinism in the dictionary, we find that this is the very thing that Darwin propagated.

Evolution, in its simplest definition *is* survival of the fittest. Evolutionary thinking has now been embraced by the egos of many Americans. This type of life philosophy has bombarded our colleges, schools, and the media. The results of this "wisdom" have been devastating. Abortion on demand, escalating murder, suicide, infanticide, sexually transmitted disease, euthanasia, violent crime, illegitimate birth, and divorce rates have soared in America ever since the nation decided that man's way was better than God's way.

For every cause there is an effect. The cause for the turmoil we're experiencing in this nation today is the result of our "survival of the fittest" mentalities. For example:

A husband and wife let themselves grow apart. Money has become more important in their lives than morals. The children stand by and helplessly watch their mother and father bicker. Finally, one day the father decides that he'll "take care of it" by calling it quits, and he files for a divorce. But for whose convenience? For *his* convenience.

A teen-age girl gets pregnant and all of a sudden her dreams for college and a bright career future seem dashed. Afraid to tell her parents and unsure of what to do, she decides to call the local abortion clinic, just for advice. And they give it to her all right.

They paint a picture for her of how a "piece of tissue" will not only disrupt her life, but will most likely destroy her chances of *ever* attaining her future goals unless she "takes care of it." So she mistakenly takes their advice, and goes in to the infanticide clinic and hands them over money so that they can "take care of *it*" for her. For whose convenience? *Their* convenience.

An aging parent gets sick and requires a life support system. But the mounting medical bills cause the family members to begin to consider having the matter "taken care of" by having the plug pulled. For whose convenience? *Their* convenience.

A pastor in San Francisco writes a book that speaks out against the sin of homosexuality. So radical militant pro-gay enthusiasts decide that they will "take care of him" and forget that killing someone is murder—which is highly frowned upon by the legal authorities! But they attempt to do so anyway. For whose convenience? The *militant radicals'* convenience.

And the list goes on...

And thus, survival of the fittest has gone a step further and now has become *convenience* of the fittest. And the proponents of this mentality are saying "Don't cramp the lifestyles of the fittest...or we'll "take care of you!"

If you are one of those who prefer for life to be, as they claim, "survival of the fittest" let me assure you that there is always someone out there who is stronger, faster, and more cunning than you...so watch out, look out, and beware!

Remember this: every effect has a cause. The teaching of that which devalues human life and causes suffering could only have come from an anti-human, anti-God source. And that source would have us believe that there is no Creator God. But now we know that to be without a Creator means that there is no set purpose, no set meaning, no set standards of right or wrong, and no set values for life itself. Then governments that are influenced by the highest bidders dictate the standards, the rights, the values...

To be without God, is to be without direction. To be without God means that we believe there is no tomorrow after this life. So simply stated, to be without God... is to be without *hope*.

Other Enemies Of The Cross

The entertainment industry, the news media, and the evolutionists aren't the only ones who are being used by Satan to deceive the people of our nation, but they're the ones I have mentioned first because their teaching lies at the roots of the problems of a selfish, lust-seeking nation. Those who believe in evolution are, by in large, trying to remove God from our society. The gay activist groups are trying to do the same. Why? No God = no conviction for offensive behavior! That's what this whole issue really boils down to.

The <u>ACLU</u>

Take for instance, if you will, the well funded American Civil Liberties Union. This is an organization that is stacked with lawyers who step up to bat in court cases for gay rights. They also go to bat for pornography, abortion, drug trafficking, violent crime, flag desecration, and atheism. These "champions of civil rights" as they like to call themselves, are trying to *force* legalized marriage for same-sex couples through the court systems. They are fighting for "equal rights" for those who are living the gay lifestyle the same way they defended the rights of African American children in 1954, but this time they aren't defending a minority because of the color of their skin. They are defending *this* minority because it is a group of people who choose the sexual act of sodomy, which is, by definition, unnatural copulation; something the Bible mentions as being right down there in the filth along with *sex with animals*!

When it comes to sexual expression of any kind, the ACLU says, in effect, "no restrictions." They oppose restraints on pornography of any kind, despite overwhelming evidence that shows that pornography leads to violent hate crimes such as rape. The ACLU even *supports* the distribution of child pornography by defending the "rights" of those who produce and market it!

The ACLU opposes police roadblocks and sobriety checkpoints. They oppose drug testing and the searching of school lockers. They have fought against the suspension and expulsions of severely disruptive and dangerous students in our public schools.

These self-proclaimed defenders of American freedoms oppose security screenings at courthouses and airports, oppose restraints on lyrics in music (even if those lyrics promote violence and hate), oppose any and all restraints on abortion, and oppose capital punishment. By defending these causes, the ACLU has actually usurped the freedoms of decent citizens and given power to the criminal and immoral elements of society.

It should come as no surprise that the ACLU defends those who desecrate the American flag. As incredible as it may sound, their founder, Roger Baldwin, was a self-professed communist who backed the former Soviet Union form of government! Their president, Nadine Strossen has written a book entitled *Defending Pornography* with the subtitle "Free Speech, Sex, and the fight for Women's Rights."

So driven by their *mis*-interpretation of the Bill of Rights are ACLU members, that they are working very hard at turning a nation founded on Christianity, into a nation of depravity. With chapters and affiliates in every state, they are not only fighting *for* these detestable things, but they are also fighting *against* all manner of Christian religious expression in public places.

Consider the following:

*From the founding of this nation until 1925, Creation was taught in schools as the origins of mankind, and evolution was not accepted. But in 1925, the ACLU (founded in 1917 as the National Liberties Bureau) challenged in court the crime of teaching evolution (it was illegal then). Although the ACLU lost the case, it remained undaunted in its pursuit of anesthetizing our nation's schools of the teachings of the Holy Bible.

* The so-called "wall of separation of Church and State" that crept into American jurisprudence in 1947, was brought about by an ACLU lawyer. The "separation" clause has been used to sway the decisions of Supreme Court Justices on other cases involving religion ever since.

*By the early 1980s, two states, Arkansas and Louisiana, had succeeded in passing laws mandating the teaching of creation science along side of evolutionary theory in public schools. But by then, the ACLU's persistence had taken its toll, and in 1987 the Unite States Supreme Court declared such laws to be "unconstitutional intrusions" of religion in the public schools.

*In the March of 1995, the ACLU sued Alabama Judge, Roy S. Moore for having a plaque of the Ten Commandments posted in his courtroom. "It's unconstitutional!" protested the ACLU. "It violates the separation of Church and State—you'll have to remove it." Judge Moore, who welcomes local Alabama clergymen to open each court session with a prayer, fought the lawsuit for several years, and although over six *thousand* people attended a rally in April, 1997 to back him and to "save the commandments," the judge deciding the case sided with the well-funded and powerful ACLU, and ordered Judge Moore to remove the plaque and stop the clergy from opening court jury selection sessions with prayer. This is despite the fact that the very first Supreme Court Justice, John Jay, specifically called for prayer to open court sessions! Judge Roy Moore stood firm on his moral convictions however, and refused to adhere to the demands of the activist judge and the ACLU. The outcome of his refusal to "recant" in the case was a positive one, and the charges were eventually dismissed.

*In February, 1996, a federal district judge sided with an ACLU lawsuit which forced the removal of a sign that said "The World Needs God" from the outside of a Montgomery County, Illinois courthouse. At first the county fought the litigation, but then the funds to stay in the legal battle with the ACLU ran out, and the sign came down—*against the will of the people* there!

*The ACLU sued the Hemet School District of Southern California for promoting abstinence-based sex education classes to its students there. The ACLU claimed that the school's view was based on "religious doctrine" and therefore violated the separation clause.

*The ACLU has sued teachers and coaches for even speaking about religion, God, or Christianity. They have sued school districts for holding voluntary baccalaureate services. They have forced the cancellation of Christian songs, prayers, and even moments of silence from graduation ceremonies. In one instance, an activist judge who sided with the ACLU, ordered that there could not even be any mentioning of Jesus, or the perpetrators would be arrested and jailed!

*The ACLU has sued the Boy Scouts of America for discrimination. The Boy Scouts crime? They won't let girls, atheists, or those who have chosen the gay lifestyle into their organization, nor will they remove the word "God" from their scout's oath!

*The ACLU has, against the will of communities, forced the removal of Nativity scenes from public places, and has for years tried to remove the word "Christ" from Christmas and rename the whole thing "Winter Holiday."

*The ACLU opposes the tax-exempt status of religious bodies.

*The ACLU is opposed to the words "One nation under God" in our Pledge of Allegiance, and would like to see the words "In God We Trust" removed from our national currency.

*The ACLU bullies and intimidates its opponents with threats of costly drawn out legal battles.

Is it any wonder that the ACLU has been called by many the *Anti-Christian* Liberties Union? This organization has distorted and twisted the Constitution to fit their own perverse agenda. They have taken the words of this national document and used them *out of context*. In fact, any astute observer knows that The Constitution does not support their views. The Mayflower Compact and the Declaration of Independence do not support their views either. In fact, *American history* does not support their views. Everything our Founding Fathers stood for opposes the actions and views of this organization. The founders, the framers, and the foot soldiers that made this country great, stood up and declared "One nation under God" not "One nation under godlessness!"

With all their persecution of Christians and protection of criminals, one may have to wonder just what the ACLU's long-range goals are. Since they fight for these things in the Supreme Court, in the State Courts, the Legislatures, and the Court of Public Opinion, just what do they want to see in America? Do they want to see the day when five-year-old Jimmy can hear the grunts and groans of his two daddies from the adjacent bedroom?

Do they want to see the day when nine-year-old Jimmy can see exactly what it is that his two dads have been doing behind those closed doors by renting an XXX-rated video from his local video store?

Do they want to see the day when thirteen-year-old Jimmy, deciding to "swing both ways" gets his girlfriend pregnant and then demands that she get rid of "it" but neglects to inform her that he has contracted AIDS due to his promiscuity with men?

Do they want to see the day when fifteen-year-old Jimmy can sell drugs to his classmates with no repercussions whatsoever?

Do they want to see the day when sixteen-year-old Jimmy can buy a case of beer, drink it, and while on his way home drive head on into a family of five, killing them all instantly...but get off the hook on a technicality?

Do they want to see the day when seventeen-year-old Jimmy, a regular porn reader, can ask his junior prom date out, then rape her?

Do they want to see the day when eighteen-year-old Jimmy, (who lives in the garage that his grandparents built for him) takes the flag that his grandparents gave to him (when he was a young boy) off its pole and into the garage where he proceeds to set it on fire? Then when his grandparent's smell the smoke and rush out and see what it is that Jimmy is doing they will yell "What in God's name are you doing?" And Jimmy will shout "Declaring freedom of expression!" Then his grandfather (a decorated war veteran) will probably say "God forbid you burn that flag you...you little fruitcake!"

The next day, Jimmy, deciding he doesn't have to put up with *that* kind of abuse, can pick up his phone and dial none other than 1-800-ASK-ACLU.

Then, I suppose, the ACLU will want to see the day when soon thereafter, Jimmy's *grandparents* find themselves in court facing invasion of privacy, religious fanaticism, and bigotry charges! And then maybe, just maybe, the ACLU will want to see the day when, finally, twenty-year-old Jimmy goes off the deep end and bombs a federal building or two. Perhaps then, in the courtroom the ACLU defense attorney can claim that poor Jimmy is a "victim of society" and circumstances "beyond his control!"

Is this the vision that the ACLU has for America? In the final analysis, if they get their way, will we see a day in America when the church bells will be silenced, and the crosses removed from the cemeteries also?

Irony Or Double Standard?

The atrocities that you have read about here are real. Before reading this, perhaps you hadn't heard very much about them. If not, perhaps it is for the reason that groups such as the ACLU don't want to have the spotlight focused on their activities, for that would reveal their true agenda. Herbert W. Titus, once a legal activist for the ACLU (who has since been converted) said this of his days with the organization: "We *invented* new constitutional rights and began to press them in courts across the nation."

The ACLU, like Disney doesn't care to have the scrutiny of the spotlight that reveals their true character and thus provides them with bad publicity. Instead, they just go about their business and continue to claim to be fighting for the freedoms of American citizens. They say they fight for freedom of speech and freedom of expression, but where are they when the people voice *Christian* expressions? On the other side of the fence with a sue-happy lawyer—that's where!

With great power comes great responsibility. The ACLU and

some other groups like them have forgotten that rights without responsibility is what leads to the moral decay of a society. The very goals that the members of the ACLU are striving to reach are setting up a system that calls for tighter government control! Isn't *that* what the members of this organization claim that they *don't* want? I think Dr. D. James Kennedy said it best when he remarked "Where character is undermined, immorality abounds. As a result, an increasingly strong government force becomes necessary to maintain order."

PAW

Another organization that has an agenda similar to the ACLU call themselves "People For the American Way." They too have been fighting hard to suppress people who wish to express their Christian convictions. Don Feder, a syndicated columnist and author of the book *Who's Afraid of the Religious Right?* is a Jewish conservative who names both the ACLU and PAW, among others, as those who "view the religious right as being the primary roadblock to the total secularization of America, and to the enactment of anti-biblical values in our laws and public institutions."

The "Top Of The Hill"

When it comes to deception, don't look too hard for the devil in your local town tavern. That, for him, would be too easy. No, instead you'll find him and his cronies working more diligently in higher places. Take for instance, Capitol Hill. There, certain members of Congress tried to push the "Fairness Doctrine" which, had it been passed, would have censored Christian television and radio ministries from our public life. Welcome to Communist America, where the hostility toward religious expression by some of our highest-ranking government officials is becoming more and more apparent!

Oklahoma Representative Ernest Istook (one of the good guys in Washington) has said that "Religious speech is being singled out and treated as if it were dangerous speech which must be suppressed by government. The only comparison is the pornography industry. If something is considered obscene, people believe that government should have the right to suppress it in advance. The only other comparable suppression is that of religious speech. It is appalling that these are being equated and treated in similar fashion."

Representative Henry J. Hyde has said that our government leaders "... have an almost schizophrenic approach to religion. We open Congress with a prayer; the Supreme Court opens its sessions with a prayer... and yet we are insistent on the antiseptic immunization of many of our public functions."

On one hand, some of our government leaders are not only suppressing the rights of Americans to express their religious convictions, but on the other, they are actually aiding and abetting the gay rights movement. In April 1997, Coral Ridge Ministries aired a documentary special entitled *Homosexuality: Your Tax Dollars At Work.* This program showed how the U.S. Government is spending more than a *billion* dollars annually to actually support the gay cause. For example, just some of the policies that have been established by the federal government include AIDS education grants to pro-gay groups and "sensitivity training" sessions for federal employees where acceptance of the "alternative lifestyle" is stressed. President Clinton signed off on this executive order in September 1993, therefore mandating an AIDS training program for the over two million workers in the federal government. The program, which is called the "Federal Workplace AIDS Education Initiative" calls for a "breaking down of audience resistance" if that resistance is based upon "religious principles."

Mr. Clinton, on one hand, has said that he has a plan to "cherish our children and strengthen American families." And in fairness to the President, he has indeed supported the V-chip, asked entertainment industry leaders to institute a voluntary ratings system, and has supported the Communications Decency Act. But on the other hand, this president has (from before the beginning of his first term in office) supported the gay rights movement at nearly every opportunity he could get. For example:

*While running for president during his first term, Bill

Clinton addressed a gay lobby group and played on the words of the late Dr. Martin Luther King Jr. when he said "I have a dream...and *you're* part of it."

Then, as President...

*He welcomed gays into the military, thus weakening the morale of our nation's armed forces.

*He appointed the White House staff position of liaison for the "gay and lesbian communities."

*He appointed a lesbian activist as assistant secretary of Fair Housing.

*He appointed over twenty other "openly gay" people to positions within his administration.

*He confirmed the appointment of David Satcher as surgeon general, a doctor who has advocated in favor of needle exchange programs for the gay and lesbian communities.

*President Bill Clinton also *quietly* revoked Executive Order #12606 on April 21, 1997, (just nine days prior to the Ellen episode) and thereby canceled a ten year policy which had been carefully designed during the Regan administration by both pro-family groups *and* Congress to protect American families from government bureaucracy. Note: It is now obvious to pro-family groups who support traditional family values that Clinton's cancellation of that executive order was a precognitive move on the part of the president to enable him to openly address and fully support the "gay cause."

*In November, that same year, Mr. Clinton became the first sitting president to publicly address a gay and lesbian civil rights organization. He did so at a dinner speech in which he urged Congress to pass legislation protecting gays from job discrimination, and thus became the first president in history to promote sexual orientation to the federal civil rights law which grants protected class status to its members. He told the gay audience of about 1,500 people that "...people who aren't comfortable yet with you need to learn to see you as fellow

Americans committed to freedom and equality." He went on to say "We have to broaden the imagination of America. We are redefining in practical terms the immutable ideals that have guided us from the beginning." The White House called the dinner speech a "community outreach gesture" and compared it to the president's participation in the National Italian American Foundation dinner. Clinton's aids played down the speech and advised news photographers in advance that they would not be able to take snap shots of Clinton meeting with Ellen DeGeneres, which he did, back stage and *out of view*. In regards to the event, White House press secretary, Mike McCurry, stated that Clinton would not follow vice president Al Gore's lead and embrace TV's *Ellen* program for its bold plot line. "That's not an area that he (the president) particularly wants to highlight," said McCurry.

*Without public debate or the approval of Congress, President Clinton also signed Executive Order 114478 into law, thus granting special rights to federal employees based upon their sexual orientation.

*In May, 1999, just one month after President Clinton issued an executive order forcing American colleges to generate data on hate crimes, the Senate Judiciary Committee heard testimony on a measure to expand federal hate crimes legislation. Two months later, that legislation passed in the Senate, and now the pro-gay lobby, which frivolously chooses to call itself a minority, has won another political battle and "sexual orientation" has now become a protected class status. This new piece of legislation, The Hate Crimes Prevention Act (HCPA), gives preferential treatment to this group of people because of their *actions* instead of the color of their skin. It also establishes a legal precedence that brings about unequal justice, and begins to punish not only actions, but *thoughts*. Clinton and others have pushed this bill through congress even though FBI statistics reveal that crimes that are categorized as "hate crimes" account for less than one tenth of one percent of total violent and property crimes.

The month of June, 1999, benchmarked the epitome of Bill Clinton's seven years of support and backing of the gay rights movement in America. During that month…

*The President backed a gay jobs bill entitled the Employment Non-Discrimination Act (ENDA). He had previously backed the same bill in 1996, but the bill was defeated by just *one vote* in the Senate that year. Congressional liberals such as Sen. Edward Kennedy (D-Mass.) reintroduced the bill in June 1999. This bill, if passed, would extend special protections to not only those who have chosen to live the gay lifestyle and are working within the confines of the federal government, but it would extend out into the general populous workplace as well. And there, if signed into law, it would elevate *sexual behavior* to the level of a civil rights category—such as race, religion, or ethnicity.

*The President placed national importance on the Stonewall riot, thus recognizing the so-called birthplace of the gay rights movement in America. By adding the Stonewall Inn (a New York gay bar that erupted in a three-day riot when police raided the bar on June 27, 1969) to the National Register of Historic Places, he became the first president ever to acknowledge a site relating to homosexual history. It is interesting to note that normally, for sites to be listed in the Register, they have to be at least fifty years old. This one was only thirty.

*The President declared that the whole month be recognized as "Gay and Lesbian Pride Month." Addressing those living the gay lifestyle, Clinton stated that he is "… proud of the many openly gay men and woman who serve with distinction in his administration, and that we should work not only to tolerate our differences but to celebrate them as well."

Note: Each year some of the most important figures in the founding and formation of our nation (such as Columbus, Washington, and Lincoln) are recognized by the federal government with a day of worthy mention (i.e. Columbus Day,

President's Day, etc.). Isn't it interesting that this president has set aside *an entire month* to the celebration of "gay pride"?

But this president has not stopped *here*. He has also taken steps to further the gay cause *internationally* as well. For example:

*He appointed a U.S. delegation to a United Nations Conference that strove for a "redefinition of the family."

*He defied the will of the Senate, and appointed James Hormel ambassador to Luxembourg; a predominately Catholic country. Hormel (a major Clinton campaign donor) openly admits to living the gay lifestyle. The only way the President could accomplish this task was by taking advantage of a rarely used constitutional provision that allows sitting presidents to execute executive branch appointments without Senate approval—when the Senate is recessing! And that is exactly what this president did. When the Senate left town for a one week Memorial Day vacation in June, 1999, Clinton jumped at the chance to fulfill his promises to the aggressive gay lobby, and he used this provision (which is historically only used in times of emergency). Hormel, who accepted the appointment by swearing in on a Bible (which was held by one of his "male partners") is a supporter of the San Francisco Public Library where the "James C. Hormel Gay and Lesbian Center" has been launched. The center has housed works that refer to pedophilia, and even bestiality! Hormel is also a financial backer of the controversial gay tolerance indoctrination video *It's Elementary*.

By reviewing all of the above, it has become clear—crystal clear—that William Jefferson Clinton has shown that he backs broad cultural reevaluation of the traditional (God ordained) roles designated for males and females in both this country, and throughout the entire world. And throughout the Clinton-Gore campaign, Al Gore has not only followed Bill Clinton's lead, he has *enforced* it. The voting public would do well to remember this.

People who believe that the Bible really is the Word of God (the ones who stand firm upon this conviction) are simply repeating what the Bible has been saying for thousands of years—that same sex perversion is wrong; that it is a *sin.* And because they stand up and proclaim it to be as such, Bill Clinton and Al Gore (and their followers) have taken notice.

Because they have taken notice, one has to wonder whether or not the complete alienation of the Christian Community is also on their agenda. What may sound like a preposterous suggestion has back of it several facts. Consider if you will the following:

*The Clinton Administration recognized the importance of Judaism to America when the President proclaimed Jewish Heritage Week in 1995, but it refused to proclaim a *Christian* Heritage Week for this country despite being petitioned by *We The People* to do so. Governors in thirty-five states have signed decrees that celebrate our rich Christian heritage, and yet the president and his followers simply said "No."

*Clinton eliminated the White House staff position whose assignment was to communicate with the evangelical community.

*Clinton has consistently granted Most Favored Nation status (MFN), now called "normal trade relations" to the Chinese Government despite these disturbing facts:
  ~Christians are being persecuted there in record numbers.
  ~Their government is *forcing* its civilian women to get abortions.
  ~Their government has allowed child labor camps to continue under deplorable conditions (to make goods for countries like the U.S. at dirt-cheap labor costs).
  ~They have imposed a forty-percent tariff on many American imports.
  ~Due to their trade barriers, less than two percent of U.S. exported goods are received there.
  ~They have been linked to espionage charges for stealing American nuclear weapons secrets.

The persecution of Christians alone should be enough to influence the President to at least impose economic sanctions against these tyrants until they stop their atrocities there. But instead, he calls them "friends." When one takes time to consider all the above, they have to sit back, scratch their head and wonder…What's wrong with this picture?

<u>N.E.A. # 1</u>: Polluting The Mind Of America

For years now, our government has also been funding the National Endowment For The Arts (NEA). This hundred million dollar government sponsored agency has produced numerous "homosexual art" demonstrations with *our tax dollars* including, but not limited to:
* Books about oral sex between women.
* Pro-homosexual TV documentaries.
* Art exhibits showing men having sex with young boys.
* A movie about black lesbians.
* A film about twelve-year-old girls who "discover" that they are "gay."
* A program depicting the sex lives of gay black men on public TV's *Point of View* series entitled "Tongues of Fire."
* Gay and lesbian festivals and dance clubs.
* Robert Mapplethorpe's works of "homoerotica."
* A crucifix submerged in urine.

And the list goes on…

So many obscene, offensive, and blasphemous art demonstrations have been funded with the American citizen's tax dollars (without their knowledge or consent) that conservatives, including some representatives in Congress, have petitioned for the complete defunding of the NEA. The House of Representatives voted to defund this program. The majority of the Senate agreed. But unbelievably, a few members of the court over-ruled the will of the American people (once again) and decided in favor of freedom of expression without regards to decency—and the $98 million dollar funding in the Interior Appropriations bill (which was signed into law by President

Clinton) for the NEA has continued on.

N.E.A. # 2: Targeting The Next Generation

The current administration has an agenda, and it doesn't exclude our children. The Congress passed legislation for a program concocted by the two-million member National Education Association (NEA) called "Goals 2000." This program, which pushes "Outcome-Based Education" has since been re-worded to "Competency-Based Education" because the educators realized that the public had caught on to this controversial teaching agenda, and decided to hide it under another name.

Teachers use to keep their sexual lives a private matter, but now those who are living the gay lifestyle are injecting their personal lives into classrooms across the nation by talking openly about their sexuality with colleagues and students at alarming rates. The concept they are using to educate our children can be summed up in one word: *re-socializing*. Their agenda is to indoctrinate our children into accepting change, and to "release" those old time-honored parental values as being "outdated."

These proponents of sex education see sex in our "modern society" as a phenomenon that is too complex for its instruction to be left up to the "varying ignorances" of parental guidance. So when it comes to Sex Education in the classroom, videos such as *It's Elementary: Talking About Gay Issues In School* have been produced to instruct educators how to talk about homosexuality in the classroom. This program, which has been endorsed by both the National Education Association and the American School Counselor Association, was produced by two women who have openly confessed that they are living the gay lifestyle. They have also been promoting this video to the Public Broadcasting System (PBS) in hopes that PBS will air it in cities all over the country. To date, over one hundred public television stations have aired the program. PBS, which is funded in part by American taxpayer dollars, has refused to air the program in some areas however. Nevertheless, proponents of indoctrinating our children with "gay tolerance" are pressing on...undaunted.

The Gay, Lesbian and Straight Education Network (GLSEN) is helping to distribute the *It's Elementary* video, and have stated that they intend to saturate the public schools with "gay-affirming lessons." GLSEN has even targeted kindergartners. As one of their spokeswomen stated "The younger you start, the better."

Groups like the Sexuality Information and Education Council of the United States (SIECUS) have also been targeting children of all ages to accept their pro-gay agendas. SIECUS has published sexuality guidelines for children from birth to five years of age entitled *Right From The Start*. Their program should be called "*Wrong* From The Start." Among other things, they say it's appropriate to teach five to eight year olds how men and women are sometimes "attracted to members of their own gender" and that they sometimes "fall in love with one another." With their widely used guidelines for sex education curricula *Guidelines for Comprehensive Sexuality Education: Kindergarten-12th Grade*, SIECUS has provided our children with not only the promotion of the acceptability of homosexual relationships, but also the acceptability of abortion, fornication, and living together out of wedlock. They also actually encourage young children to masturbate.

Another group of gay activists that has been trying to "educate" our children calls themselves Parents, Families and Friends of Lesbians and Gays, or (PFLAG). PFLAG believes that sex education should be introduced to children very early in life. They also claim to believe that scientific evidence bears out that a person's sexual orientation is not subject to modification. One of PFLAG's recommendations to its members is to pressure the Boy Scouts of America to allow those who are living the gay lifestyle into that group's highly respectable and integral organization. On August 4, 1999, after a lawsuit had been filed on behalf of a dismissed scout leader who "came out of the closet," the New Jersey Supreme Court ruled in favor of PFLAG that the Boy Scouts' ban on gays was illegal (under New Jersey's anti-discrimination law) and the Boy Scouts were forced to reinstate the scout leader.

The Clinton Administration is, of course, backing many of

these groups. At the recent White House conference on "hate crimes" held at George Washington University, the president and several Cabinet officers (who had already set the goal of indoctrinating America's children) endorsed a K-12 plan to teach children to be tolerant of, among others, "homosexuals." According to Los Angeles Times syndicated columnist, Cal Thomas "As part of this new federal intervention, the departments of Justice and Education will be sending 'anti-hate crime resource guides' to your local school district." Thomas went on to say "This latest, but probably not last, effort by the government to reprogram the minds of our children must be resisted. Concerned parents are wasting their time trying to reform a corrupt system. Parents should reassert control over their children's lives by pulling them out of the government schools. They should see that their children are educated according to their values and beliefs, teaching them the truth about history and every other subject the schools once taught but have now mostly abandoned."

Cal Thomas was exactly right. The Clinton administration's Department of Education (DOE) has indeed now released a report entitled *Protecting Students from Harassment and Hate Crime: A Guide for Schools*. This new guide lists several pro-gay organizations as resources.

Yes, in our public schools today, our children are being taught evolution. In our public schools today, our children are learning to accept the gay lifestyle as "normal" and some are even having condoms handed out to them! In our public schools today, our children are being denied the teaching of God's Word, Creationism, and our Nation's rich Christian heritage, and are even having their homework censored if it even mentions Christianity. In October 1996, for example, a Tennessee ninth grader named Brittney Settle got a zero for writing a research paper about Jesus Christ. Brittney's teacher said it was "not an appropriate topic for public school." Brittney's classmates were allowed to write about witchcraft, demons, reincarnation, and magic, but Jesus Christ "wasn't appropriate." Brittney then sued to have the grade removed from her record, saying her freedom of speech had been violated. The Supreme Court, however, upheld the zero! The Court stated "...schools have the power to control student speech related to curriculum." And another little girl, ten-year-old Genny LeDoux, of Kaplan, Louisiana, who, when assigned to write a story about Easter wrote about the resurrection of Jesus. When she received her paper back, the teacher had crossed out every reference to Jesus Christ and God, and had replaced them with "Peter Rabbit."

It's a sad day in America when public schools permit our children to write about witchcraft, demons, and Peter Rabbit, but make Jesus Christ "off limits."

Activist Judges: The "Untouchables"

It seems to me, that if I were the devil, I would focus most of my energies on the destruction of the traditional family unit. In doing so, I would be striking at the heart of that which keeps people in touch with their Father in heaven. Logic tells me that this is exactly what is happening today. Satan is using people in positions of power to accomplish his goals. Take liberal federal judges for example. From the Supreme Court on down to the district courts, federal judges have the power not only to pass judgment, but to establish policies as well, and none of them are elected by the people, they are appointed by the President and approved by the Senate. And when they are appointed, they are appointed for *life!* Some of these presidential appointees are reshaping our society through laws and policies that fit their own viewpoints and agendas. They are literally making up their own versions of the law.

From 1972 through 1978, over twenty states repealed their laws against sodomy. But even so, in many states in this nation as well as in many other countries, it is still *illegal* to commit acts of sodomy. However, within the past few years, several notorious decisions have been rendered in opposition to the will of the masses. In Colorado for example, a majority of voters approved a law in 1992 banning special rights for those who are living the gay lifestyle, but in 1996 it took just *six* Supreme Court justices to overthrow the ban! The same thing happened in Cincinnati, Ohio. These were just two of the more publicized battles that took place that turned out courtroom decisions that were travesties of justice.

It was with the backing of President Clinton, that a group of federal judges overturned the long-standing policy of excluding "homosexuals" from the military when they implemented a "Don't ask, Don't tell" policy instead. They did this despite opposition from the overwhelming majority of our military commanders, such as Colin Powell.

Ruth Bader Ginsburg, is a Supreme Court Justice (who use to be an attorney for the ACLU), and is a modern feminist. She co-authored a report in 1977 for the U.S. Commission on Civil Rights regarding "Sex Bias in the U.S. Code" in which she declared that the wording in the code be changed. Regarding that which constituted a sexual offense with a minor, she suggested that the age of the child be changed from 15 to ... less than 12 years old." She also voted against bans on special rights for those who are living the gay lifestyle, and has declared the all-male enrollment of the Virginia Military Institute to be "unconstitutional." That institution must now accept females. Could the NFL (National Football League) be the next target on her agenda?

Like two sides of the same coin—both the increasing of gay rights and the decreasing of Christian rights—have been stepped up in recent years by federal activist judges. Like the ACLU, these folks are attempting to remove the freedom of religious expression, especially *Christian* expression, from nearly every vestige of our society. Since 1962, numerous Supreme Court decisions such as Engel (1962), Abington (1963), Stone (1980), and Edwards (1987) have forced voluntary school prayer from our public schools. The Court has even ruled against prayers at schools graduation ceremonies, calling them "unconstitutional."

Equal treatment bills for teaching Creationism along side of evolution were introduced in fourteen states in 1980-81, and became laws in Arkansas and Louisiana. But federal judges declared both laws "unconstitutional" in 1982. As mentioned earlier, Louisiana appealed to the Supreme Court, but in June of 1987, the court ruled 7-2 against the laws, stating that they "transgressed the separation of church and state."

On June 25, 1997, the majority of both the House and the Senate passed the Religious Freedom Restoration Act (RFRA), which would have provided American citizens protection to freely express their religious convictions, by a vote of 532-3. But the bill was simply canceled by the Supreme Court! This was nothing less than a travesty of justice and an indisputable mockery of God by the handful of members of the Supreme Court who voted against RFRA.

Supreme Court federal judges also decided that a 103-foot tall cross located at a San Francisco public park (which had stood there for 63 years) had suddenly become what they called... "unconstitutional."

The Communications Decency Act was passed in Congress in 1997, but it too was rejected by seven out of nine judges in the Supreme Court. Thus the Court dictated its own will over the will of our elected members of Congress (who represent the will of *millions* of American citizens), and now pornography runs rampant on the Internet *under the law*.

The highest court in our nation has now also ruled that "At the heart of liberty is the right to define one's own concept of existence, of meaning of the universe and the mystery of human life." By making this statement, six Supreme Court Justices have basically ignored the Declaration of Independence which lists certain rights that are gifts from God, such as the right to life, for one. This ruling was in *Planned Parenthood vs. Casey*, and these words have quickly become known as the "mystery passage" because they undermine moral absolutes and make all of our laws based on relativism (one's own interpretation of right and wrong). It also suggests that human rights are no longer gifts from the Creator, but are gifts that are either *allowed* to citizens or *usurped from them* by the Supreme Court. The latter of the two is exactly the opposite of what the Supreme Court is supposed to be doing! It's supposed to be defending the will of the moral majority, and handing out justice based on the unalienable rights that are mentioned in the Declaration. In this decision, once again just a handful of liberal activists, *just six people*, undermined religious liberties in our nation.

Rulings like those I've mentioned here are also happening at the lower court levels as well. The U.S. Court of Appeals for the Ninth Circuit for example, decided that a large cross that had been erected by the American Legion (as a war memorial) in Eugene, Oregon had to be removed due to its "religious symbolism."

In the city of Stowe Ohio, no one had a problem with the city seal there—which had remained intact for many years—until recently, when the ACLU made the Court there aware that the seal contained an item of "religious symbolism."

In July 1999, hate crimes legislation was passed in the U.S. Senate. Prior to this, the mere mentioning of this new legislation had already begun to affect court decisions across the nation. In Wisconsin, for example, David Ott, a man who formerly led the gay lifestyle but has since received Christ as his savior, merely tried to verbally convince another man to abandon the gay lifestyle, and as a result was sued by that man and charged with disorderly conduct! The normal fine for such an offense there would have been $500. But since Ott had "discriminated against a homosexual" the so-called hate crimes "penalty enhancer" upped the punishment, and Ott found himself facing a possible year in jail and a $10,000 fine! Ott settled the case, but was ordered by the activist judge there to attend "sensitivity training," perform fifty hours of community service, and was placed on probation for one year! Ott's legal costs to defend himself mounted to $7,000. All this happened to this man because he told another man that he would be better off with Christ than with homosexuality!

Less than a hundred years ago, our third president foresaw the problems of the federal judiciary. He called it "an irresponsible body" that "...works like gravity by night and by day, gaining a little today and a little tomorrow, and advancing its noiseless step like a thief, over the field of jurisdiction, until all shall be usurped from the states." He wrote that "...the opinion which gives to the judges the right to decide what laws are constitutional, and what are not, not only for themselves in their own sphere of action, but for the legislature and executive also, in their spheres, would make the judiciary a despotic branch." Today, this very thing is happening.

It has now become apparent that the high courts of our land have been given too much power. As Constitutional lawyer and founder of Prison Fellowship Ministries, Chuck Colson has rightly stated "America is now being ruled by a runaway judiciary."

The IRS: Using *Your Money* To Fund The Gay Agenda

The Internal Revenue Service is suppose to utilize the money that they obtain from the American tax-paying citizens for the betterment of America, but they too have now joined in on the financial backing of the rapidly expanding gay rights movement in America today. In November 1997, GLOBE (an affiliation of Gay, Lesbian Or Bisexual Employees in federal government service) held a pro-gay conference in which IRS employees were paid by *your* tax dollars to attend. The IRS authorized taxpayer dollars to be used to pay for "administrative leave" to those employees who attended the conference stating that it "furthers diversity objectives."

APA #1: Have They Lost Their Minds?

The American Psychiatric Association (APA) is another organization whose leaders have, in the past, decided to support the gay cause. In 1973 the APA removed homosexuality from its list of psychiatric disorders, an action that significantly aided the gay rights movement. Then they went as far as to categorize homosexual behavior with that of the rest of society in general. They began using terms such as DD Up and DD Down, which stand for "Defining Deviancy Up" and "Defining Deviancy Down." What they are saying is that when deviant behavior becomes prevalent in society, then society tends to define deviancy down, or lower its standards in order to get along. Defining deviancy up takes what was once the accepted norm in society and re-defines *it* as deviancy!

In 1994, this organization also revised its Diagnostic and Statistical Manual of Mental Disorders by declaring that in order for someone who desires pedophilia (sex with children) to be considered to have a mental disorder, that person must have "clinically significant distress or impairment in social, occupational, or other important areas of functioning."

The APA would have us believe this garbage is acceptable. But the thing that they are not telling us is that deviant sexual behaviors (homosexuality and pedophilia) have *not* become prevalent in our society by any means. One report after another indicates that only one to two percent of our society claims to be living the "gay" lifestyle. Has the APA forgotten the other *ninety-eight* percent?

<u>APA # 2</u>: Dispensing Junk Science

The American Psychological Association (not to be confused with the above APA) is an organization that has now went as far as to say that child molestation is no longer a big deal—as long as it is consensual! This APA released a 3-author report in July, 1998 in its *Psychological Bulletin* that stated, in part, that pedophilia should not be classified as "abuse" simply because it is generally viewed as immoral. The report said that terms such as "child abuse," "molestation," and "victims" should be replaced with *value-neutral* terms such as "adult-child sex." As unbelievable as it may sound, the report suggested that sometimes when an adult has sex with a child, that it is a "willing encounter," and that it can even have "positive" effects. The North American Man-Boy Love Association (NAMBLA), a homosexual-pedophilia activist group, applauded the APA report on its website as "good news." NAMBLA is a group that has been working diligently to have laws against pedophiles dropped from the books.

Unbeknownst to most American citizens, gay activist groups such as NAMBLA, from all over the world, are working hard to lower the age of consent laws. Ever since 1972, when the National Coalition of Gay Organizations adopted their "Gay Rights Platform," one of their major goals has been the repeal of *all* laws that govern the age of sexual consent. In Britain, for example, the federal government there lowered the age of legal sexual consent from 21 to 18 around five years ago. In 1998, a fight in the British parliament was underway to lower the age to 16. In Canada, they lowered the age of legal sexual consent to just 14, and in Holland they went to 12.

<u>NOW</u> : The Re-emergence Of Ancient Gnosticism

By now, you can surely see that there are those who are imposing a radical viewpoint upon the rest of society and teaching people to think differently; to think as they themselves do. The National Organization for Women (NOW) is no different. The leaders of NOW have officially endorsed the gay rights movement, and have battled anti same sex marriage legislation in around forty states.

If one takes a hard honest look at history, they begin to see that modern feminism (the driving force behind NOW) is nothing more than a re-emergence of the ancient religion of gnosticism. This was a cultic religion in which women focused on giving themselves over to self-pleasures. Their "religion" took them into the lesbian orgies and to the point of worshipping both female deities and *sex* itself! The Gnostics, whose religion was derived from a blending of Greek philosophy and Eastern Mysticism, believed and taught that there was no such thing as "sin" and that women were superior to men. Today, we can see ample evidence of the re-emergence of this type of doctrine when the president of NOW, Patricia Ireland, goes on TV and tells the members of her organization to stand staunch against organizations such as Promise Keepers (PK)...whose only intentions are to serve God and to be better husbands and fathers!

Both the high rate of divorce and the lesbian movement have sprung up in this country today as a result of the push for modern feminism by groups such as NOW. None of these things are new however, except that the terminology has changed and that these things are now happening in *this* country.

By *NOW* it should be clear to see that movements such as these all have one thing in common: they are meant to destroy God's design for the human family structure ...through *deceit!*

Other Followers

Other (once dignified) organizations have also decided to

follow the lead that President Clinton and the groups that have been mentioned here have been setting forth. The FBI, for example, for the first time ever, is now admitting those who are living the gay lifestyle into their once highly respectable bureau. Even the United States Department of Agriculture (USDA) has gotten in on the act, and has added "sex orientation" to its nondiscrimination policy.

As you have seen, this type of mindset is even pervading the business sector of America. When large business organizations such as *United Airlines*, *American Airlines*, and *Bell Atlantic* place their advertisements in gay magazine publications—what type of message are they sending? When *AT & T* sponsored one of the largest gay and lesbian festivals, as they did recently in Washington—what were they trying to say? When *Mellon Bank* made the statement that it would not do business with pro-family groups such as Focus on the Family due to Focus' outspoken Biblical viewpoint on homosexuality, what were they trying to prove? (Interestingly, Mellon retracted their unethical statement after receiving numerous phone calls from upset business patrons.)

America is not the only country falling from grace because of the aggression of gay rights activists. In fact, She is lagging behind the "advances" that have been made by some other nations. Within the international movement to push for gay acceptance, three major developments have occurred recently. First, in 1995 the Supreme Court of Canada ruled that "sexual orientation" is comparable to race, gender, or ethnicity. The Court, therefore, provided those living the gay lifestyle with special minority status. Then in May 1999, the Canadian Supreme Court ordered the provincial government there to redefine the term "spouse" to include "same-sex partners."

The second thing that has occurred recently that is creating ripples and beginning to affect "tolerance levels" throughout the international community, happened in the Church! Hundreds of bishops from churches affiliated with the Church of England worldwide attended the Lambeth Conference, the main forum for debate among Anglicans. During that conference, those living the gay lifestyle requested that their role in the church be changed. The so-called "Lesbian and Gay Christian Movement" released a book of open letters urging a reconsideration of the Anglican Church's traditional teaching on homosexuality. This caused division within the Church there, and is now affecting the ideology of some members of other churches as well.

The third major development pushing for unconditional acceptance of homosexuality world-wide occurred when around 130 youths from over a hundred countries signed off on a "sexual rights manifesto" during the 1999 United Nations Population Conference. That manifesto suggests that children, as young as *ten*, should have the legal right to have sex with anyone they choose.

It's All About Rhetoric

Throughout this writing, the author has purposely refrained from the casual use of the terms "homosexual" and "lesbian" when referring to *people* who are caught up in the sin of living the gay lifestyle. The reason for this should, by now, be obvious. When we use the same terminology that those who are promoting the acceptance of this sin are using, we fall into the same thing that they have—deception. Then we are playing into the hands of the enemy (Satan) because, as we have seen, he uses deception tactics to fool people into sinning against God.

When it comes to deception on a mass scale, one of the Evil One's main tactics is using our own vocabulary terms against us. But when Christ shines the light of the truth on *words*, we can see their *true meaning*. Christ clears away the mist. He lifts the fog of sin that has blinded us to the truth. We can then see that...

The word "homosexual" is, in fact, a person who perverts the structural and functional use of his or her sexuality through unnatural sex acts with members of the same gender.

The term "hate crime" is, in fact, an all-inclusive term that describes nearly *all* crimes that are committed. Even the casual shoplifter tends to "hate" the system under which he or she lives. They rebel against it, and steal from those who have used the system more wisely.

The term "hate speech" is, (outside the obvious lowering of one's self by trying to demean a person because of the difference of their ethnicity) in fact, an attempt by politically corrupt organizations and individuals to further the gay rights agenda by *silencing* all opposition to the sin of sexual perversion—a sin that will keep people from entering into the Kingdom of God.

Indeed, Satan is using the vocabulary spin-doctors to further *his* agenda. And, even though our president has refused the request of the gay lobbyists for homosexual marriages to be enacted into law, we may be inclined to ask this question: "In what direction are the President and the other leaders of this nation taking us in regards to our traditional family values?"

When terms such as *"value neutral," "sexual orientation," "re-socializing," "alternative lifestyle," "domestic partnership,"* and *"adult-child sex"* are being used....when statements and policies such as *"defining deviancy down," "sensitivity and diversity training," "breaking down of audience resistance," "Don't ask, Don't tell,"* and *"redefinition of family"* are being made by the powers that be....we may also be inclined to ask the question: "Is America being duped?"

For Every Effect—A Cause

For every effect, there is a cause. The cause of the gay rights movement in America today *is* deception on a mass scale. And back of all of this is spiritual wickedness in high places. {Ephesians 6:12}. Satan and his followers have been working diligently through our very own satellite technology to deceive us. Yes, welcome to 21st Century America, where mind control has been taking place for over twenty-five years now, but has just recently begun to pick up the pace! Now, with the use of the most powerful and influential mediums ever known to man—TV and Radio—the Prince of the Power of the Air has been providing us with more and more "information" and more and more people are falling victim to the lies that are being fed to them through these propaganda and censorship machines.

Scientists tell us that for every effect, there is a cause. When people are trying to decide what they want in life, their values determine their motives. And what determines values? *A person's values are determined by material which enters their mind to the point where it reaches the subconscious level.* Some of this material is voluntary. Some of it is involuntary. Note well here, however, that the way in which an individual responds to this material is self-determined; *it is a choice.*

The motivating factor is one link in a chain of factors that determine an individual's chosen lifestyle. In other words, *material* that reaches the subconscious mind determines *values* that determine *motives* that prompt a person into *actions*, which determine that person's *lifestyle*. The eventual outcome depends most largely upon the material (input) to the mind at the beginning of the chain. Notice:

Input—>Values—>Motives—>Actions = Lifestyle.

Evolution, pornography, the bias views of the entertainment and news media, liberal government agendas, and modern feminism...these are bombarding our senses daily! They make up the very mortar that has been used to lay the bricks that serve as the structure for the lifestyle of homosexuality, which some people find themselves trapped in. These are the elements—the links in the chain that binds them. They serve as the foundation for their lack of faith, and therefore, their way of life.

"Goals 2000"

Around ten years ago, *Time* magazine published *Beyond the Year 2000: What to Expect in the New Millennium.* Its predictions for the family (as we know it today) were bleak. Under a section entitled "The Nuclear Family Goes Boom" the editors of the magazine predicted the demise of the traditional family unit! They predicted that divorces will be "normal" and that multiple marriages or "serial monogamy" will take the place of the "once thought to be normal" nuclear family.

As we work through the 2,000th year anniversary of the First advent of our Lord Jesus Christ, the more outspoken of the gay communities will become more and more intent on destroying the traditional family structure of America. But when their agenda is pointed out, they will say that there is no such "agenda." They will say that they just want to be able to live together and love one another the same way straight couples do. They will also say they have been victims of social intolerance and racial discrimination. What they won't tell us, however, is that the majority of those who live the gay lifestyle engage in *promiscuous sexual behavior,* and that the average life span is now only 42 for men, and only 45 for women as a result of sexually transmitted diseases...such as A I D S.

But promiscuity is nothing new. Like we find written in that dusty old biblical book of Ecclesiastes, "...there is no new thing under the sun." It is a sin that has been around for a long, long time. It found its way to the Greek Island of Lesbos where the famous poetess Sappho lived at around 600 B.C. The word "lesbianism" is derived from that place. Sappho wrote love lyrics directed toward women. Several of her poems refer to Aphrodite, that voluptuous pagan goddess of love who had many *male* lovers. Perhaps Sappho too had more than one sexual preference and her share of lovers, for she was at one time married and even had a daughter.

And so we see that promiscuity is nothing new. And even though it may have been around on Lesbos in 600 B.C., or in America in A.D. 2000, or everywhere and every time in-between, God's Laws against it have not changed. They are relevant for all ages, and all times. His word states so. And in that word, God clearly states that he designed the family to be a holy union between a man and a woman and their children, and nothing that the gay activists, the biased media, the liberal judges, or even the president or vice-president can say or do can change *that.*

And the great dragon was cast out,
that old serpent,
called the Devil, and Satan,
which deceiveth the whole world:
he was cast out into the earth,
and his angels were cast out
with him.

{Revelation 12:9}

Chapter Three

A DIVIDED SOCIETY

The Choice

choose you this day whom ye will serve...

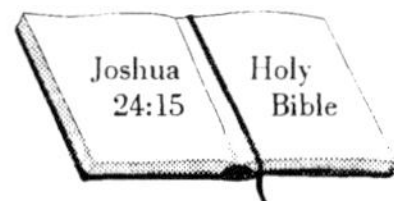

GOD IS THE ORIGINATOR OF HUMAN SEXUALITY. He created the family structure when he ordained the union known as marriage. He also gave us the proper order in which we are to progress in our human sexuality. First comes love, then marriage, then (and only then) sex. If you doubt that our society has not been victims of brainwashing, then ask yourself this question: How many people today are getting *that* in the right order? In the Bible, fornication (sex outside of marriage) is called sin, and it is forbidden. Same-sex perversion is not only forbidden, it is cursed! But now the groups that you have read about here are trying to get us to believe that it is *normal* and should be acceptable.

God's Design For The Family

God designed mankind after his own image—far above the animals, and he told the first man and woman on the earth to be fruitful and to multiply. Animals have sex. They multiply, but they do not band together in a union that is meant to be life-long; a union that is even called "holy" (matrimony). Even Christ, who often quoted from the Old Testament, said "Have you not read that he which made them at the beginning made them male and female? For this cause a man shall leave his father and mother and shall cleave to his wife and they shall become one flesh. Man must not separate then, that which God has brought together." {Matthew 19:4-6, Mark 10:6-9}.

Today, man is trying to separate what God has created as the design for the family unit when he tries to get all of society to accept same-sex unions the same as opposite-sex unions.

The Fifth of the Ten Commandments states that we are to honor our father and our mother so that our days will be long upon the land, which the Lord has given us. {Exodus 20:12}. Can a person claim to be honoring his parents when gay sex acts are more akin to the animal plane than the human plane of sexuality? Remember this, Christ said "Go and sin no more." A man is, if converted by Christ, an heir of the family of God, not just another animal.

The "Gay Gene"

In an attempt to justify this sin, many of those who support the gay lifestyle are now claiming that a person can be "born gay." For years scientists have been searching for a genetic link to homosexuality, but none have been able to confirm any biological differences between gays and straights. In 1993, *Science* magazine released an article that supported the finding of a portion of DNA that supposedly confirmed some people's belief that they were born gay. They based the article on the findings of a gay activist named Dean Hamer, a researcher with the National Cancer Institute. The magazine has since renounced its earlier publication however. On April 23, 1999, *Science* reported that after studying more than fifty gay male siblings, researchers concluded that their data did *not* support the earlier claims made by Hamer. There have been other chromosomal studies attempting to isolate genetic factors that would indicate a predisposition of a homosexual orientation at birth, but they too have all been utter failures as well.

Just A Theory?

The gay gene theory is more than just a theory however, it is a *hope* on the part of those who choose to be gay to have their feelings of anxiety, guilt, and remorse removed by the discovery of something that does not exist. God would not make a person gay, then condemn that same person for being what he created them to be. That would make no sense at all. Nevertheless, the search for the so-called "gay gene" goes on... but only by those who have a vested interest in finding a reason to excuse themselves from engaging in or promoting this type of debauchery.

American Psychological Association Executive Director, Dr. Raymond Fowler, has stated that "Medical and mental health professionals know that sexual orientation is not a choice and cannot be altered. Groups who try to change the sexual orientation of people through so-called 'conversion therapy' are misguided, and run the risk of causing a great deal of psychological harm to those they say they are trying to help." But according to *Masters and Johnson* reports, as well as others, those living the gay lifestyle can indeed change their sexual preference to heterosexual. For those who disagree with these findings and cling to the gay gene theory, some serious questions arise. For example:

Q.   Why do some prison inmates engage in homosexual or lesbian behavior only while they are in prison? By the way, if those on the receiving end of their behavior do not concur, it is called *rape*. Imagine that.

Q. When released from prison, why do nearly all "homosexuals" or "lesbians" return once again to heterosexual (normal—not deviant) relationships?

Q.   How can homosexuality be the result of a biological trait when many people who were once living the gay lifestyle have since found freedom from their sin through Christ?

Q.   Because they have been converted back to normal monogamous heterosexual lifestyles, do these people not serve as living examples to the transforming power of Jesus Christ?

Q.   And what about bisexuals—those who *choose* to have sex with members of *both* sexes—such as Anne Heche, who was living a heterosexual lifestyle before she met Ellen?

If these questions are looked at honestly, their answers make it clear that homosexuality is not genetic, but simply behavioral.

The Issue Of "Acceptance."

As we have seen, over the past decade pro-gay activists have, with the support of the liberal biased media, created a trend that calls for the social acceptance of *that* which was once considered so immoral, so detestable...that writers of the past could not even mention the word! Today, those who are crying out the loudest want us to accept them as "who they are." They do not want the focus to be placed on what they *do*, but instead on who they *are*. Why? Because what they are *doing* is *wrong*. Make no mistake, sin is sin—nothing less than willful violation of God's Laws.

One thing that the pro-gay activists don't seem to understand is that love (true love) *is* discriminating. It does not discriminate against people, it does, however, discriminate against actions. True love calls for discernment. True love calls for us to abhor that which is evil, and to cling to that which is good. {See Romans 12:9}.

To love wrong is to sin. Those living the gay lifestyle are *living in sin.* They are cohabiting in willful disobedience to their Creator's design for their lives. Homosexuality is sin just as lying, cheating, stealing, adultery, and murder are sins. It is a well-known fact that many thieves, adulterers, and even serial killers have tried to "justify" their sins, and be accepted by society as well. Many in the gay community will undoubtedly lash out against this statement. But is it so wrong? Sin is sin, and *all* sin is so terrible in the eyes of our Holy God that it is punishable by death! And we are *all* sinners! Each time we willfully disobey God, we *are* sinning. At those times when we become weak and fall into a temptation, we should *immediately* repent of it. We should hate our own shortcomings; we should by no means flaunt them.

Outside of God's redemption, the main difference between someone who receives God and someone who rejects Him, lies in their *attitudes*. One has faith in God, the other lacks that faith.

One understands that his Creator has every right to do what He will with his creation, the other is like the clay that rejects the very Potter that makes it. One strives to live according to eternity, the other according to the ephemeral things of here and now. One places little confidence in the flesh, the other places all confidence in the flesh—even to the point of worshipping it. One knows that even though he has sinned, there is still hope for him to be reconciled to God through Jesus Christ, for Christ paid the penalty of death *for* him, and said "Go and sin no more." The other, lacking this faith, not only lives in sin, but also tends to boast about it. In doing so, how can he expect Christ to propitiate him before a perfectly Holy and righteous God?

Victims Of Social Intolerance?

As they march down the streets during one of many gay day parades acting in the usual profligate manner, activists hold signs up high that declare their need for "justice." *"Intolerance," "Hate Crime," "Homophobic,"* and *"We Are All God's Children"* are waved back and forth for all to see. A hidden agenda tells them that they need to proceed in such a manner as to appear to be "victims" of social intolerance and injustice. It also tells them that Christians are narrow-minded judgementalists. So they hold onto the idea that Conservative activists must be "bigots," "hate mongers," "religious zealots," "homophobes," and "extremists" who are "threats to civil liberties." On the other hand, they consider themselves "idealists," "social liberals," "family planners," "feminists," and "defenders of freedom and the American way." A good example of this type of thinking can be seen in a response by Elizabeth Birch, the executive director of the Human Rights Campaign (HRC). A bill that pro-family advocates felt they needed in order to protect the sanctity of marriage being defined as that between one man and one woman only, was introduced on Capitol Hill and called the Defense of Marriage Act or (DOMA). In response to this new piece of legislation, Birch enthusiastically voiced her organization's contempt for the bill and called it the "...wedge-driving, bile-filled, mean spirited, really, really stupid so-called Defense of

Marriage Act." Apparently she has never read the 34th verse of the twelfth chapter of the Gospel of Matthew.

Today, in this nation there are times when some people go to say a prayer at a graduation ceremony, post a plaque of the Ten Commandments in their courtroom, demonstrate in front of an abortion clinic, or read a bible in the breakroom during a work lunch hour or on the school bus on the way home, and they are told "You can't do that." Then, there are other times when "art" exhibits featuring men having sex with young boys, or a crucifix of Christ submerged in urine are displayed, and no one is suppose to protest. What happened to "We are all God's children?"

Homophobic Rhetoric

Several years ago, someone coined the term *"homophobic."* And now this word is brought up in debates over special rights for those who are living the gay lifestyle. For example: in May 1995, the U.S. Sixth Circuit Court of Appeals rejected an earlier lower court ruling pushing for gay rights in Cincinnati, Ohio. The court stated that gays are not entitled to special protections under civil rights law, as are minorities such as women or African Americans. Shocked and outraged by the outcome, the trial attorney for the "Equality Foundation of Cincinnati" which brought the suit, stated in the *Cincinnati Post* that the court's decision was "stunning in its homophobic rhetoric."

A "homophobe" is what gay activists tend to call anyone who speaks out against homosexuality. They claim that those who don't understand gay people are fearful of them, and therefore tend to have "homophobia." They invented this word as a way to make it sound as though any person who speaks out against homosexuality should be considered as someone who has a psychological neurosis. In other words, a portion of that two percent fraction of our society (who are caught up in the gay lifestyle) is telling the rest of us that anybody who is not tolerant of sexual immorality and speaks out against any efforts to confuse the gender identity of the nation's children is, in effect, a person with an emotional disorder!

The 1980 version of the Random House Dictionary makes no

mention of the word "homophobia." It does, however, list the word "homophile." The two definitions given for *that* word are (1) a homosexual person, and (2) advocating the civil rights of homophiles: a homophile organization. This word "homophile" has the ring of the word "pedophile" to it, and Random House has since dropped it from its dictionary. They have, however, now added the word "homophobia." The definition they give for "homophobia" is "an unreasonable fear or hatred of homosexuals and homosexuality."

After reading the above, this author has to wonder if this means that we should now start calling someone who speaks out against adultery "adulteraphobic" too! I doubt it though. Those who design the dictionaries won't include that word—it wouldn't be politically correct.

The Real Victims Of Intolerance

Robert H. Knight, Senior Director of Cultural Studies for the Family Research Council has said that the gay rights movement which is using methods of coercion is "...perhaps the most powerful political and social force per capita in America today"...and "It poses the greatest threat to religious freedom that this country has ever seen." And I believe he's right. As gay rights activists become more and more aggressive, the only stumbling block that besets their path is the courageous outspoken biblical viewpoint of conservative Christians.

We are now seeing the bulldozer of a pro-gay agenda trying to plow over any and all opposition. In 1997 for example, after watching Ellen's infamous "coming out" episode, the Christian singing duo Angie an Debbie Winans wrote a song called "Not Natural." The lyrics of the song state that this type of lifestyle is "not natural." Shortly after their song hit the airwaves, condemnation from gay activist groups began to bombard the Winans.

In 1998 several other public figures felt the heat—the backlash of severe criticism—as well when they voiced their Biblical-based convictions that homosexuality is a sin. For example, all-star defensive end for the Green Bay Packers, Reggie White, who is the NFL's all-time leader in quarterback sacks and is also an ordained minister, was invited to give a motivational speech in by the Wisconsin Legislature. White's speech called upon society to band together to reverse the degenerating state of our nation, and he called homosexuality a sin. The intolerance toward his speech was not immediate, but when gay rights advocates, bias secular newspapers, radio talk shows, and politicians learned of White's speech, they jumped all over him both verbally and in print. As a result of the picketing of *CBS Sports* by gay activists, *CBS* announced that they were backing out of their reported $6 million application with White as a sports commentator! The *Campbell Soup Company* snorted that White's comments were "inconsistent" with their fundamental ethics, and they declined to renew his contract as one of its spokesmen as well.

Mississippi Senator Trent Lott was another example. He received condemnation from media and pro-gay groups as well for his answer to a question asked of him on the Armstrong Williams TV talk show. On the show, Lott was asked if he believed that homosexuality is a sin, and he replied simply "Yes, it is." He then compared it to other addictions such as alcoholism. House Majority Leader Dick Armey, a representative from Texas, echoed Lott's views. "I do not quarrel with the Bible on the subject." Armey told reporters.

In response to these public proclamations of homosexuality being a sin, President Clinton's press secretary, Mike McCurry told reporters that statements like these were "backward in their thinking" and that "...those who think as Senator Lott do are the reason it's hard to get anything accomplished in Washington!" He also said that Lott's comment was "ignorant." The Human Rights Campaign said Lott's remarks were "out of step with the American people." Is it not strangely interesting that this man, whose name which just so happens to be "Lott" is being criticized and condemned by angry homosexuals?

HRC also said they were "deeply disappointed and angry" with the comments made by Reggie White. They went on to say "...we believe religious disagreements do not justify discriminatory statements that seek to demean gay Americans and divide this country." HRC was speaking from one side of the tracks however, because on the other side those who simply spoke *the truth* in love, such as Reggie White, were being called "homophobic," "stupid," and "nigger" by so-called human rights activists.

Others are suffering for their outspoken views on the sin of homosexuality as well. For example, a social worker was fired for refusing to place foster children with a gay couple. In 1996 a sports commentator named Ben Wright was also fired (by *CBS)* after he made what gay activists referred to as an "intolerable remark" about two male golfers. And as mentioned earlier, due to the provision of the hate crimes penalty enhancer, David Ott suffered injustice for his outspoken views as well.

Ralph Reed, the past executive director of the Christian Coalition, has said: "We live in a country where one out of every three children is born out of wedlock, one out of every two marriages ends in divorce, one out of every three pregnancies ends in abortion, and one out of every four high school students drops out of school without graduating. Murder is the leading cause of death for African American males aged eighteen to thirty-four, and a minority adolescent male living in our nation's capital has a higher likelihood of being killed than an American soldier did in Vietnam. And yet, there are still some who believe that the most frightening thing that could happen in America is for people of devout faith to become involved in public life."

When the mentality of a group of people is that there are no moral absolutes and Christians are seen as the bad guys...when they twist the word *tolerance* to fit a perverse agenda...when they flaunt sin in front of children as they march down the streets fondling one another...when they shout lewd comments out in front of the churches...then that group of people has lowered themselves into the dregs of society. There simply is no good excuse for their behavior because it deteriorates the very soul of our nation. I think President Ronald Regan summed up this whole issue of "intolerance" quite adequately when he said "The frustrating thing is that those who are attacking religion claim they are doing it in the name of tolerance, freedom, and open-mindedness. Question: Isn't the real truth that they are *in*tolerant of religion?"

Should Society Tolerate Lust Of The Flesh?

Our society has had to learn the hard way about the improper use of sex. First it was fornication, and what did *that* unbridled use of sex provide us with? A nation where venereal diseases run rampant, where thirty percent of all pregnancies end in abortion, and thirty percent of our children are born out of wedlock.

Then came adultery, the willful violation of the Seventh Commandment. And what did *that* provide us with? A nation divided in half; one where at least fifty percent of all of our children are being raised in single parent or step-parent homes. Many even have step-step-step parents and relatives because their parents (by blood) just can't seem to get their priorities straight, nor can they stand by their convictions or commitments. Instead, they just let their libido's prevail unchaste.

The impact of divorce on our children has been devastating, but our society has come to tolerate fornication and adultery regardless of the tragic results, and now it wants us to tolerate homosexuality. And what has *that* provided us with? AIDS: the disease for the hopeless. It's called Acquired Immune Deficiency Syndrome, it has no cure, and it is spreading across our nation at rates that even the most astute observers are probably underestimating. It is, as stated by its title, *acquired.* How is it acquired? Overwhelmingly through sexual contact, especially through promiscuity (acts of lust of the flesh). And even though the AIDS virus continues to spread, the gay activist groups keep on promoting the gay lifestyle, and have now even begun to promote bisexuality as well. They are calling for an annual celebration that recognizes the history, culture and community of bisexuals.

God warned us about such things thousands of years ago, but many still refuse to listen. And now, even the holders of the two highest positions in our nation are telling us to accept the sexual sin of sodomy as "normal." Since the vice-president feels that the American people should be "forced" into accepting homosexuality, we may be inclined to ask "What's next?" Will we be forced into the acceptance of pedophilia?

So far, our society (as a whole) is still intelligent enough to realize that it can not tolerate the pedophile, at least not by law...yet. The outlandish act of child molestation is how the pedophile fulfills the desires he holds *in his mind* to satisfy the lusts of the flesh and to control somebody else. But to the pedophile, it's just nature running its course. Since they supposedly evolved from the primordial slime, it's just their animal nature that makes them rape children, right? Why doesn't society tolerate such an act? Because it is *wrong*. It is twisted, perverted, and abhorrent. There's no way around it—pedophilia, pederasty, homosexuality and bisexuality are sexual perversions—they are at enmity with God's design for human sexuality, and the Word of God speaks of them as detestable sins. When the Bible predicted our society of today, it called it a society in which wickedness is tolerated by the leaders, by the legal and educational institutions, by the media, and even by the churches!

The Church Divided

Yes, even in the churches today we are feeling the effects of division among those members who rebuke same-sex perversion, and those who welcome it under the guise of tolerance. During a ten-day Episcopal General Convention held in Philadelphia recently, presiding Bishop Edmond Browning said "It was Jesus, not me, who said there would be no outcasts."

In March of 1998, a senior pastor of a large Omaha Methodist church, the Reverend Jimmy Creech "committed" two women to each other. A heated battle within the church ensued, but a slight majority ruling found the pastor innocent of violating church policy by performing the ceremony. The jury fell just one vote short of a guilty verdict. And in speaking of why the national United Methodist Church should accept those who are openly living the gay lifestyle, the Reverend John Schwiebert has said "The church just needs to give people room to be who they are." In the autumn of 1999, the 60-member board of the United Methodist Church even went as far as to call for the end to all discrimination against those who are living the gay lifestyle. They also called upon the Boy Scouts of America to change its oath and current membership policies by allowing gays into their organization. The Church said that they will support the efforts of Lambda (a national legal defense organization fighting for full recognition of "gay civil rights").

The First Episcopal Church's St. Mark's Cathedral also recently became the first of its kind to admit a dean who openly professes that he is living the gay lifestyle. Due to the efforts of gay and lesbian lobby groups such as "Officials of Integrity" the Episcopal Church has, through its accommodation to be "more compassionate" pushed its "no outcasts" propaganda to the point where its membership has *declined* by over thirty percent in the past thirty years. Now that's irony for you, or perhaps a more fitting word would be *retribution*. Officials of Integrity are intent on achieving their major goal of having the 2.5 million-member church accept same-sex marriages. But many bishops within the church have already declared that if same-sex marriages are accepted that they will break away from the church. Bishop James Stanton said this: "Do we change the Ten Commandments to make them more palatable to people? The more accommodating we become, the more we drive people out of the church."

The Presbyterian Church is another denomination that is having similar problems. The stated clerk for the 2.7 million-member Church, Reverend James E. Andrews, filed a brief with the Supreme Court on the Amendment 2 Colorado case that stated that the Presbyterian Church disapproves of homosexual behavior, but such activity should be "treated as matters of private conduct." Opinions and views such as this are causing divisions in this church as well.

To those church leaders who have adopted the view that compassion and acceptance is more important than the laws of God and his set standards of right and wrong, may I call your attention to the most popular Christian writer of the 20th Century, C.S. Lewis, who said "If no set of moral ideas is better than any other, there would be no sense in preferring civilized morality to savage morality, or Christian morality to Nazi morality." And as R.C. Sproul has said "If you strip God of *any* of his attributes, you are committing idolatry."

Yes, we have a loving god. And yes, we have a forgiving god. But we also have a god who *judges* sin, and is the One and only true God: the God of the Bible. We need to worship Him—not a god of our own making. Any church that claims to be Christian, but at the same time embraces homosexuality, has fallen away from true Christianity, and into apostasy. If the members of those Churches doubt this, I challenge them to write a book on this subject of homosexuality, using the *entire* Bible as their only source of reference.

Christ Came To Divide...

When Jesus Christ spoke during his first earthly ministry, he did not gain the favor of everybody. Being put to death on the cross is not an award for "political correctness." Jesus simply spoke the truth, and let the chips fall where they would. His words caused a division among the people of his day, and they have been causing division among people ever since.

Christ, in speaking to his servants said "Ye are my friends, if you do whatsoever I command you." "...for all things that I have heard of my Father I have made known unto you." {John 15:14-15}. And he went on to say "If the world hate you, know that it hated me first."{verse 18}. And in speaking of those who are "of the world" he said "If I had not come and spoken unto them, they had not had sin: but now they have no cloak for their sin. He that hateth me hateth my Father also. If I had not done among them the works which no other man did, they had not had sin: but now have they both seen and hated both me and my Father." {John 15:22-24}.

Which brings us to this point. Did Jesus condemn homosexuality? Many writers who promote the gay lifestyle say "no." In fact, they say that Jesus said nothing whatsoever about the matter in the Bible. But anyone who knows the *whole* Bible knows that Jesus said "Think not that I came to destroy the law, or the prophets: I did not come to destroy, but to *fulfill*. For verily I say unto you, till heaven and earth pass, one jot or one tittle shall in no wise pass from the law, till all be fulfilled." {Matthew 5:17-18}.

The laws given to Moses by God in the Old Testament clearly

condemn forbidden sexual practices such as homosexuality. Jesus walked in the ways of his Father, God, and instructed us to do the same. He even said "...He that hath seen me hath seen the Father." {John 14:9}. "...I am in the Father, and the Father in me." {John 14:11}. and "I and *my* Father are one." {John 10:30}. Being one with the Father, who forbids men to lie with men, clearly indicates that Jesus also condemns the sin of homosexuality!

At his Second Coming, Christ will bring peace to this world. But from his first ministry until the time of his return, Jesus Christ came to bring division into this world, not peace! Many people will be surprised, if not shocked by this statement. It is, nevertheless, true. He said so himself. {See Luke 12:51-52}.

...The Sheep From The Wolves

When Jesus spoke of himself as being the good shepherd, he also spoke about people and how they are divided into two groups. One group follows the shepherd, the other comes to steal, kill, and to destroy. Those who are engaged in the so-called "liberal social movements" of today are teaching false doctrines to others through their own rejection of supernatural Christianity.

Jewish syndicated columnist, Don Feder, had this to say about the matter: "The divide in America isn't Catholic, Protestant, Jew; it's between people who believe in biblical morality and people who are opposed to it. For instance, those who think that a marriage is a man and a woman versus those who think marriage could be two men or two women or several individuals or between a brother and sister or what have you." Feder believes that the true extremists in America are those who are opposed to biblical morality, and he's right.

As we have seen, even many church members are feeling pressured by certain groups to compromise their values, but the Bible warns us to reject their humanistic views. Having a form of godliness, they reject the power thereof {2Timothy 3:5}, and we are warned to avoid them. As Henry M. Morris, founder of the Institute For Creation Research put it "We cannot escape being taught doctrine from somewhere. If we will not receive true doctrine from God's word, we will inevitably become indoctrinated with the world's humanistic deceptions, for these impinge upon our thinking continually..."

When we look at the Big Picture, we cannot help but notice that we are indeed living in a divided society. We live in a nation where human rebellion is lashing out against God, and against human hope. We live in a nation where those who reject the gospel have pitted themselves against those who profess it.

...The Hopeful From The Hopeless

The hopeful are those who try to obey the laws of God, are ready to give an account for the faith that is in them, and above all, rest their hopes in the life, death, resurrection, and second coming of the Lord, Jesus Christ, and the new world order he will bring with him.

The hopeless, on the other hand, are those who have placed all their desires, all their dreams, all their energies, and all their trust in the ephemeral material world that we live in today.

The hopeful fear God, and as a result try to live by his laws. They realize that the Ten Commandments are still the rules of conduct that make for happy living. They also realize that humans cannot break the Commandments, they can only *break themselves* on them, if they disobey them.

The hope*less*, on the other hand, could care*less*. Many of them claim they don't even believe there is a God. They are a disrespectful generation of people who give little, if any thought to God's Laws for their lives. Instead, they live only to satisfy their lust for earthly pleasures.

The hopeful know that they were once in the same situation as are the hopeless—on the road to ultimate destruction! But they let Christ take their blinders off so they could see the ugliness of their sin. The hopeless refuse to even listen to the gospel message. In ignorance, the hopeless have even branded labels on those who are trying to follow after righteousness (as we have seen). Today, when we hear them mention the "Far Right" and the "Liberal left" they don't even realize that the Bible spoke of them many years ago when it said "A wise man's heart is at his right hand, but a fool's heart at his left."

{Ecclesiastes 10:2}. It also said "When the Son of Man shall come in his glory, and all the holy angels with him, then shall he sit upon the throne of his glory and before him shall be gathered all peoples, and he shall separate them one from another as a shepherd divides his sheep from the goats. And he shall set the sheep on his right hand, but the goats on the left." {Matthew 25:31-33}.

His Divine Mission

Each person either surrenders to their *sin*, or surrenders to *Christ*...there is no in-between ground to stand on! So are you one of those who follows after the good shepherd? Or, are you one of those who has come to steal, kill, or destroy? If you are resisting Satan, he will flee from you, and you already know which group you are in. But if you are defiling your body temple through acts of same-sex perversion *without remorse*, then you belong to the second group because you are literally destroying your soul! And just remember this: Satan is the "shepherd" of that group, and he is leading his "sheep" to the slaughter!

Yes, Christ came to divide, but first he came to *inform*. He also came to save and to restore humanity by destroying the works of Satan. He will ultimately judge the wicked and heal the broken relationship between God, The Father, and that remnant of mankind that he so chooses.

Chapter Four

GOD'S ANGER REVEALED

The Facts

And the Lord shall be seen over them, and his arrow shall go forth as the lightning: and the Lord God shall blow the trumpet, and shall go with whirlwinds of the south.

THE BEGINNING OF WISDOM IS FEAR OF THE LORD. That is why I will preach with admonition, but without compromise. The message here is not like the messages being put out by many others today, for it does not conform to society in order that it may by accepted by it. As spokesmen of doctrinal integrity, we must alert people who choose the gay lifestyle that the choices they are making are placing them in great danger both in the present physically, and what is even more important, in the future, spiritually.

A wise man once said "It is fit and becoming in all people, at all times, to acknowledge and revere the Supreme Government of God; to bow in humble submission to his chastisement; to confess and deplore their sins and transgressions in the full conviction that the fear of the Lord is the beginning of wisdom; and to pray, with all fervency and contrition." Who was that man? Was it John Wesley? No. Perhaps it was Martin Luther. No. How about one of the Popes? No, it wasn't one of them either. Well it had to be a man of the cloth, right? No. That man was the sixteenth U.S. President, Abraham Lincoln, and *he* did not compromise the word of God for political gain. The Bible is clear, you cannot compromise with the world for it is void of the truth. So this writing is not a watered-down doctrine. Instead, it is like good medicine that is given full strength in the hope that it will make the believer well again.

Those Who Repudiate God's Word

As we have seen, many outspoken people who are living the gay lifestyle commonly question the authority of the Bible. They say that it was written by men who based their writings on ancient traditions and superstitions. Many even believe that the Bible is just a bunch of stories that were written to amuse their children! But the Bible is none of these. In fact, the Bible itself (as you will see in a later chapter) contains so many proofs of its infallible accuracy that any critical eye would have to confess that it indeed could only have originated from one source—*God.*

One warning laid out in the Bible can be found in the fifth chapter of the Old Testament book of Daniel, where we read of the account of King Belshazzar of the Chaldeans. Now because of the circumstances surrounding this king's life, he must have heard about God's laws, but he, like so many before him, simply refused to listen. So King Belshazzar threw a big party where he and his party-going friends worshiped idols of false gods. They also carelessly drank wine from some of the golden vessels that had been taken from God's sacred temple. During the party, the fingers of a man's hand appeared out of nowhere and began to write a message on the wall of the king's palace. King Belshazzar was so troubled by what he saw that his knees began to knock! No one at the party could read or interpret the writing on the wall, so the king called for the wise men of Babylon to try to read and interpret the message, but none could. Finally someone told the king to call upon the Judaean exile, Daniel, who had been known from the past to have interpreted dreams. Daniel said the message was from the One and only true God. Then Daniel told King Belshazzar that the message said that his kingdom had been numbered by God, and that it was finished. Because he had refused to acknowledge God's word, King Belshazzar was slain and his kingdom fell...that very night!

Not Willing To Listen

Many living today would consider the Biblical account given above to be nothing more than a fable. Many in the gay communities refuse to consider that such things may actually be true. But as we have seen, they also refuse to accept the reality of Satan. Nevertheless, there are battles taking place in and around our world—in that spiritual realm that is hidden to the naked eye. An example of this can also be seen in the tenth chapter of Daniel. There, we are given the account of a heavenly messenger who appeared to the prophet Daniel. This messenger (or angel) told Daniel that from the time that Daniel had set his heart upon understanding God's will (Daniel had humbled himself and had been fasting for three weeks) that his prayers had been heard, but that the "prince of the kingdom of Persia" had withstood the messenger angel for 21 days. This scripture passage points out that there was a battle taking place in the spirit realm in and around Daniel and the government of Persia. The chief angel Michael even came to help the messenger angel in his battle against the evil angel who was shadowing over the Persian government at the time. {Daniel 10:12-13}.

Now I did not write this book without knowledge of how some people who have chosen the gay lifestyle think on subjects such as the Bible. Of the several that I have been acquainted with, two individuals come readily to mind. Being the curious fellow that I am, I went to great lengths to pick their minds to find out *why* they feel the way they feel. Many respectful conversations were held, but in the end, the sad conclusion that I had no other choice to reach was that they were *unwilling* to listen to what God's word has to say on this subject.

The first individual I encountered was an acquaintance of my friends from their work. John even became a friend of mine. We knew John for years, and although we knew he wasn't a very manly type, we never suspected that he was living the gay lifestyle. Finally, one day John "came out of the closest" when he confessed to one of his work associates. We were shocked! To that point, John had always been a conservative type of fellow. He displayed a good attitude, dressed casual, and maintained a high level of self-discipline which showed up in his ability to go far in his profession. But after John's "coming out" he *changed*. His choice of clothing became radically different; his attitude changed, and his self-discipline practically deserted him as he began to have sexual relations with both men *and* women.

I always liked John, I never hated him, even to this day. He was always a personable chap. After we found out about his secret, I tried to talk to him. We had many conversations about his choice of lifestyle. After many attempts to "convert" John back to heterosexuality, I realized that he was not going to change. During many of our conversations, I would mention (as tenderly as I could) what God's word had to say about the subject, but John had the tendency to say "Maybe your God says that, but my God says..."

John believed that he could not change, and he would refer to how *his* god was a loving and forgiving god who "would not have created him to be gay, and then turn around and punish him for being that way." Although there was some truth in his words, John failed to accept one important fact—that there is but *one* God, and he is a god who is true to his word. In other words, John refused to believe that his actions were the result of his own choices, not his genetic makeup.

The second person that was struggling with this same problem was Bernie. I worked at a job along side of Bernie, and once again, there were many "conversations" with some even turning out to be heated debates! Bernie would tell me "I *can't* change." And in response to that I would say to him "Take the "t" off of "can't" Bernie!" And Bernie, being a very outspoken, outgoing, and friendly fellow to most people, once said "He [God] is going to have to answer to *Me*, because I can't help being who I am!"

But I would ask of Bernie, or John, or any other person who believes that they are incapable of turning away from this sin...

Can a *person* judge *God?*

I know that a person *can* change, and *can* turn away from sexual immorality, for I too was once enslaved to my lust of the flesh, but only for women. The Apostle Paul once said that he was "Chief among sinners" ...but that was only until *I* came along! But like the apostle Paul (and many others), I have since been blessed by God to see the error of my ways and to go to him in prayer and confess my sins and ask for his help. He has indeed helped me, for I am no longer steeped in sexual immorality, but now live for Christ, and to do *his* will. I won't say that there are still not temptations, for as with all people, I still have my share. But I have learned, through the word of God, that it is not a sin to be tempted, but it *is* a sin to flirt with the temptation. I have also learned that flirting with sin invariably leads to succumbing to it, for the mind is always seeking an outlet for the desires it stores up.

I think that what this whole issue really boils down to today, as well as throughout all of history, is that those who engage in sexual sin do not fear God the way that they should. Instead, they live in defiance of Him. It's not that a person can't change, it's that they *won't* change. It's a matter of *will*, and therein lies the difference.

One of the most prolific minds that the Lord has blessed us with was that of Benjamin Franklin. Franklin once said this: "...since He [God] has given us reason whereby we are capable of observing his wisdom in the creation, he is not above caring for us, being pleased with our praise, and offended when we slight him, or neglect his glory."

Indeed, God is offended when we slight him! The carnal mind *is* at enmity against God for it is not subject to the law of God, neither can it be. In other words, those who live in the ways of the lust of the flesh cannot please God unless they *change*, and live in the ways of the spirit instead. The Bible says that to avoid fornication, let every man have his own wife and let every woman have her own husband. It does *not* say let every man (or even some men) have his own husband. Nor does it say let every woman have her own wife or "domestic partner" or "live-in lover" or what have you.

In the second epistle of Paul to the Thessalonians, the Bible also predicted the eventual outcome of those who will not listen. Written therein, the apostle warned that there would come a day when those of sin would be revealed, they would be sent strong delusion, and with all deceivableness of unrighteousness in them that perish; because they received not the love of the truth that they might be saved. {2Thessalonians 2:10}.

It should also be interesting to note that the only mention of "tolerance" in the Authorized King James Version of the Bible is found under the word "tolerable." It is used to describe how it will be more tolerable for Sodom and Gomorrah and for Tyre and Sidon in the Day of Judgment than for the cities that refused to pay any attention to the deeds of Christ, or receive or even hear the words of his apostles. {See Matthew 10:15, 11:22-24, Mark 6:11, and Luke 10:12-14}. Today, gay rights activists have exploited the word tolerance to further their agenda. They are using it to defend their position against those who are speaking out against this sin. But the true followers of Christ are speaking out just the same. In the tenth chapter of Luke, in the sixteenth verse, Christ said "He that heareth you, heareth me; and he that despiseth you, despiseth me: and he that despiseth me, despiseth him that sent me."

Those unbelieving cities who reject the Word of God and refuse to even listen, will suffer an even greater condemnation than did those immoral cities that were destroyed in the past, for the "...Scripture cannot be broken" said Christ. {John 10:35}. Indeed, the words of God stand true and firm—for *all* times.

Warnings From The Past

Once again, God is serious about sexual impurity! He even gives a list of those who will not enter into His Kingdom by reason of their wickedness. Sexual immorality, indecency, lust, evil passions, and greed are among those vices that will bring God's fierce anger and ultimate judgment. The Bible even clearly reiterates this statement several times. People who are living the gay lifestyle are putting their lust for the flesh before God, and as a result have become worshipers of a false god (wrongful sex). But the Word of the Living God tells us to let no one deceive us with their vain words because the wrath of God comes upon the children of disobedience. Over and over again, the Bible explicitly warns us to keep the statutes of the Lord, for there are great rewards that await those who keep them, and great punishments reserved for those who *will* not!

How similar the people of America are today to the Israelites of long ago. God rescued that nation from tyranny, only to watch them choose the way of sin over his laws of righteousness. As a result, He punished them.

The Puritans sought a godly lifestyle. They were of the Christian faith. So God brought them over to America not only to escape religious persecution and the tyranny of British rule, but also to light the torch of freedom for all those who sought to live after the Laws of God. They were a band of travelers who derived from a single church, and God brought them over safely on the Mayflower despite the trials and tribulations that they endured. God even destroyed a man who was trying to shake their faith during the voyage! He then preserved their generation by sending them an Indian guide to help them survive in the wilderness of the "New World." As the years passed, He gave them prosperity because they strove to live by biblical mandates.

But as usual, with the passing away of time, there seems to come the passing away of good judgment. After several generations, disrespectful and unlawful people had crept in to that once godly body of people.

By the time the 20th Century had come along, the "modern thinkers" of the day had begun to place money before the Almighty. So God let America go her own way, and do her own thing. As a result, America began to reap the rewards of her harvest, and in 1933 she suddenly found herself on the verge of a complete economic collapse because...THE JUDGMENTS OF THE LORD OUR GOD ARE TRUE AND RIGHTEOUS ALTOGETHER!

The country was, as Franklin D. Roosevelt said, "dying by inches." But President Roosevelt saw the Big Picture, and under his direction, the country did an about face. It was during his First Inaugural Address to the nation (which had just entered the Great Depression), that Roosevelt said "The only thing we have to fear is fear itself...We face arduous days that lie before us in the warm courage of national unity; with *the clear consciousness of seeking old and precious moral values.*" (Emphasis added).

Roosevelt was president during both the Great Depression *and* World War II. On January 25, 1941, he inscribed a prologue to a special edition New Testament published by the Gideons, which was distributed to the American soldiers as they left for service during the war. It said:

> "As Commander-in-Chief, I take pleasure in commending the reading of the Bible to all who serve in the armed forces of the United States. Throughout the centuries men of many faiths and diverse origins have found in the Sacred Book words of wisdom, counsel and inspiration. It is a fountain of strength and now, as always, an aid in attaining the highest aspirations of the human soul."

During the darkest hours of World War II, after having described the United States as "The lasting concord between men and nations, founded of the principles of Christianity," Roosevelt asked the crew of the American Warship to join him in a rousing chorus of the hymn "Onward, Christian Soldiers."

Ever since then, we have been reaping the rewards and benefits of the sweat, tears, and bloodshed of those who toiled long to preserve this great nation. But now, just a few generations later—like fattened calves awaiting the slaughter— we once again find ourselves in a nation that has begun to "wander in the wilderness" because of its sins.

The Danger Inherent

When one generation of people does not diligently teach its children the *word* of God, then that nation can suffer very quickly the *wrath* of God! In the first chapter of the epistle that the apostle Paul wrote to the Romans, Paul describes the fate of those people who chose sexual immorality over the Holy God of the Universe. In the letter, Paul states three times that God "gave them up"...to uncleanness {verse 24}...to vile affections {verse 26}...and to a reprobate mind {verse 28}. These statements by the apostle bring us to this point. There seems to be a recurring theme throughout history that goes like this: First,

God blesses a society because they put him first and foremost in their lives. As time goes by however, the society begins to forget who it is that has been blessing them. They then even begin to remove God from their lives altogether. With the built-in need to worship, they then turn to false idols (anything that takes the place of God in their lives). Sexual immorality then moves in, and people begin to stoop lower and lower. Fornication runs rampant, and homosexuality becomes the last debase action that God seems to tolerate. God then removes his grace from that society and *gives them up* to Satan. The society then collapses and is ultimately destroyed as a result of its own sin!

In some instances, we have seen that the destruction of wickedness comes from the hand of God himself. He punished Adam and Eve by removing them from paradise! He wiped all but one family off the face of the earth with a great deluge! He scattered the human race all over the planet by mixing up their language when they mocked him by trying to build a tower that would reach into the heavens themselves! He rained burning sulfur down on the wicked cities of Sodom and Gomorrah! He struck down the pride of the once mighty nation of Egypt with plagues of bloody water, frogs, gnats, flies, dead animals, boils, hail, locusts, darkness, and the deaths of their first-borns, and finally had to drown their armies in the Red Sea! He killed twenty-three thousand disobedient Israelites in one day for *sexual immorality*, and broke the stubbornness of the rest of them by sending them to wander in the wilderness for forty years! He brought down thousands of idol-worshipping Philistines with the mighty strength of just one man—Samson! He used a mere humble boy named David to defeat a giant and take down an army! And, He instantly snuffed out the lives of a husband and wife who tempted the Holy Spirit when they deliberately held back money from, and then lied to the Apostles of Christ!

As punishment for their disobedience, God has removed his loving kindness and protection from whole nations, and has let not only plagues, droughts, and famines come upon them, but also terrible wars. These things were written as examples for others, and as a warning for *US*, that we should not lust after evil things—as they did.

Will *we* heed the warnings of the past? Or, will that degenerate part of our society that prefers Satan as their King convince the rest of us that their way is better than God Almighty's? Then when our land experiences turmoil, should those who have neither said, nor done anything in opposition to this evil, wonder why?

I believe that the only reason that this country is still experiencing the blessings of God is that there are many here who still believe that God *is* who he says he is. They are still maintaining their faith. There is even an uprising of those in the Christian Community as was demonstrated by the over million man turnout of Promise Keepers who stood in the gap in Washington, D.C. in 1997, and prayed. There, at our nation's capital, men of many different colors, races, and even religious backgrounds got down on their hands and knees and humbly repented of their sins before the living, holy God.

The Holiness Of God

The Holy God of the Bible wants to have a relationship with mankind. So in the Old Testament, God spoke to man in order for man to know the difference between holy and unholy, and between clean and unclean. He spoke to man and instructed him to teach future generations all the statutes that he had spoken to them through his servant Moses. But because of the weakness of man to sin, man defiled himself, and therefore alienated himself from his holy Creator. It took the first coming of Christ (as mentioned in the New Testament) in order for man to be "reacquainted" with God.

In speaking of the creation of man, the Bible states that God created man in his own image. In Genesis 1:26 we read these words: "And God said, Let *us* make man in *our* image, after *our* likeness..." (Emphasis added). When combined with the Gospel according to Saint John, Bible scholars agree that in Genesis, God the Father was speaking to his son (Jesus) during the creation of man.

Although he was created in the image of God, the first man called Adam sinned and fell short of God's glory. Therefore the progeny of Adam inherited a "sin nature," and unlike God, who is holy, man became unholy. As time passed, man also became unclean and ungodly.

The Defilement Of Man

The "Book of books" has much to say about man's *defilement*. Throughout its pages we are told of how man defiles himself not by things from outside of him that enter into him, but rather by those things which come out *of* him. Earlier you read about how the outside material that reaches an individual's subconscious mind determines (to a large degree) that person's lifestyle. But understand this, most of that material is permitted to enter the mind through the conscious decisions that are made by the individual. The powerful subconscious mind is mostly influenced through repeated doses of things that are mixed with feelings or emotional content. In other words, a man is not defiled from the outside in, but from the inside out! It is through the profane things by which his mouth speaks, through his unclean living habits, and through the violation of his chastity that a man makes known the defilement of his heart, his mind, and even his conscience! The Bible tells us of how man has defiled his garments and the very land he lives upon. We are told of how man defiled God's holy tabernacle, his holy sanctuary, his holy temple, his holy day, and even his holy name. But we are also told that when that great city, the Holy Jerusalem, descends out of heaven from God, that there shall in no wise enter into it any thing that defileth, neither whatsoever worketh abomination, or maketh a lie: but they which are written in the Lamb's book of life. {Revelation 21:27}.

Jesus: More Than Just A Man

After his ascension, many things were written about Jesus, of which the most reliable are found in the Scriptures. John the Baptist, the greatest man who ever lived that was born of human parents said he was unworthy of even unloosening the lachet of Jesus' shoes. {See Matthew 11:11 and John 1:27}. Here was the most holy man alive, or who *ever* lived (outside of Jesus) saying he was "unworthy." Why? Because John understood who Jesus was.

He also understood that even the lowest in the realm of heaven is greater than the highest in the realm of earthly flesh.

And so now we begin to understand, we begin to see that this Jesus was *more* than just a baby lying in a manger, *more* than a man who gave his life for others, *more* than a great prophet, and *more* than one who died on a cross. The Bible tells us to behold the Lamb of God that taketh away the sin of the world! It also tells us that the "lamb" is Jesus Christ, who *is* the eternal Word of God, whom through all things were created! He existed in the very beginning, at the right hand of God, the Father, as his only begotten son! Eternal and majestic, full of grace, beauty, truth, justice, and *holiness*, Jesus Christ (the spotless lamb of God) shed his immortal god form and traveled down from the highest heaven to the lowly earth to become the seed of a woman, and then the light of the world! Who, being in the form of God, thought it not robbery to be equal with God (a member of the Godhead), but made himself of no reputation and took upon him the form of a servant and was made in the likeness of a man who humbled himself and became obedient unto death, *even* the death of the cross. {Philippians 2:6,8}.

And so now we can finally see, now we can finally understand the truth! The truth of the incredible significance this man, this *god* has had in the history of the world, and in the ongoing affairs of humankind! This Jesus shed his godly perfection and donned human imperfection in order to communicate with people on their own level, and to pay the debt of sin for humanity. When he was finished, he ascended back up into heaven where he now presides *once again* at the right hand of the Father, preparing a place for those who believe upon him and confess his name, and preparing also for the day of judgment for those who do not. {Proverbs 30:4, Hebrews 8:1, Revelation 3:21}.

A Name Above Names

Jesus is known by many names in Scripture. In the beginning, he is called the Word (Logos in Greek) because he is the one who articulates or speaks the will of God. He speaks, and *it is done.* {John 1:1, Revelation 19:13}. He is known as Yahweh (in Hebrew), which is Lord (in English). During his first earthly ministry, he called himself "The Son of God," "I AM," "The Son of Man," and the "Good Shepherd." He was called "Emmanuel" (which means *God is with us*). He was called "Master" and "Rabbi" (meaning *my teacher*) by his disciples. The multitudes that went before him shouted "Hosanna to the Son of David!" (Blessed is he that cometh in the name of the Lord) and "Hosanna in the highest!" {Matthew 21:9}.

Jesus was also called "Messiah" (a Hebrew title meaning *the anointed one*). This particular title was given to the promised Saviour, whose coming was foretold of old by the Hebrew prophets. "Christ" (in the Greek) means the same thing. He was, *and is* the "Prince of Peace" {Isaiah 9:6}, and the "firstborn from the dead." {I Corinthians 15:20-23}. He was simply called "Nazarene" by those who did not understand who he really was.

Jesus Christ is the mediator of the New Covenant. He is also the Rider of the White Horse of Revelation. Written therein, he is called "King of Kings" and "Lord of Lords." {Revelation 19:16}. He is also referred to as the "bright morning star." {Revelation 22:16}. Great in power and majestic brightness, He has been given authority over both heaven and earth, and is the only one who is worthy to break the seven seals and open the scroll described in this great prophetic book. No one else but Jesus, in heaven or on earth is worthy to do so. {Revelation 5:1-9}.

Being holy and true, Jesus has the key of David, and he opens and no man shuts, and he shuts, and no man opens! The Book of Revelation also says that there are (or shall be) one hundred and forty-four thousand redeemed of mankind, of whom all are virgins because they kept themselves pure from sexual relations and have never told lies. These "faultless ones" all follow after the holy Jesus Christ faithfully. {Revelation 7:4, 14:1-5}.

Yes, Jesus is the first and the last, the beginning and the end, who is and was and is yet to come! The Scriptures also call him Wonderful, Counselor, the Mighty God, and the everlasting Father. It is *He* who will be the one *true* Supreme Court Judge of all of mankind on Judgment Day. {Revelation 19:11, 20:13}. Having heard all this regarding the greatness and the holiness of Jesus Christ, the "Son of the Most High" it behooves us to fear God, for Christ said "*...my Father is greater than I.*" {John 14:28}.

Yes, glory be to God in the Highest, whose very name is so Holy that mankind was fearful of uttering it, and rightly so, for *HE* standeth in the congregation of the mighty; and judgeth *among* the gods! He sits on his sacred throne and rules over the entire universe! And this God does not call us to live in uncleanness, but in holiness, after his own image. Whoever rejects his teaching is not rejecting man who proclaims his gospel, but the Sovereign God The Father himself, who gives his students his Holy Spirit. For it is *HE* who has lifted up the authority of his son, and placed his name above every other name in heaven and on earth, so that in honor of the name of Jesus, every knee shall bow and openly proclaim that Jesus Christ is Lord. {Philippians 2:9-10}.

Created In HIS Image

As you have read, God created the first man in His *own* image. He then saw that the man needed a companion that would be more suitable than the animals that had also been created. So He caused the man to fall into a deep sleep and He removed one of the man's ribs and formed the first woman from it. {Genesis 2:21-24}. This is something the modern feminists have a very hard time dealing with, and yet the very word "woman" literally means *taken out of man*. So God formed the first woman as one of man's own kind, with bone of his bones, flesh of his flesh. God created the woman knowing that she would fulfill both the man's emotional and physical needs. Today, when a man shacks up with a man, or a woman with a woman—in order to try to fulfill these needs, they're barking up the wrong tree. The tree of life is over at the end of the *obedience* orchard.

Why A Sexual Issue?

After God had formed them, he then told these first parents of the human race to be fruitful and multiply. Therefore, God had ordained the union of man and woman; husband and wife, who were to bear children and cover the earth with them, and this is where sex comes into the picture.

Sex is clearly one of the focal points mentioned throughout

the Bible. It is mentioned in both positive and negative terms. It has the power to create as well as the power to destroy. The proper use of sex is for the perpetuation of mankind within the proper family unit. It was undoubtedly also created for both man and woman's pleasure. But when sex is used outside of these boundaries, though it may contain temporary pleasure, what always follows is *pain.* Pain such as that which is felt from break-ups, divorce, unwanted pregnancies, abortion, or sexually transmitted diseases (STD's). These things result in the ruining of one's reputation, loosing self-respect, hurting loved ones, feelings of guilt and anxiety, sickness, sorrow, and yes, even death!

Wrongful sex seems to be the epitome of rebellion towards God. Because God is holy, and because he ordained the family structure, those who despise him tend to rebel against his authority by engaging in acts of *un*holiness. When used in a deliberate act of perversion—such as homosexuality—sex is probably the most intense form of idol worship and paganism that there is. As we have seen, the worshipping of sexuality is not just a modern phenomenon. Sexual orgies have always taken place at the height of idol worship ceremonies. The most notable example being the practice of Baalism that took place in ancient Israel. Baalism was the deification of immoral passions. Within that system of worship, the people burned their children as sacrifices to appease a god that didn't exist—so that they could engulf themselves in sexual fetishism.

How tragic and how sad was their state of affairs! But are we much different today? In the city of San Francisco today, they have reopened the "bath houses" where people go to have same-sex orgies. Is a nation where people do not only this, but can legally sacrifice their children (on the altar of abortion), really that much different than ancient Israel was?

One thing we can be sure of is this—those who do these detestable things, and then preach their form of "tolerance" will find out that God is only tolerant for so long...then he *acts!* As we have seen, He destroyed those who did these things at the foot of his holy mountain, and he destroyed those who did the same in those wicked cities such as Sodom and Gomorrah.

Christ: A Consuming Fire!

You have read about the warnings of the past. Now read about the warnings of the *future*. Although God is merciful and long-suffering, he will not remain silent forever. The Holy Scriptures state that in the final days perilous times shall come. For men will be lovers of their own selves, covetous, boasters, arrogant, blasphemous, unthankful, unholy, and *without natural affection*. They will be disobedient to their parents. They will be truce-breakers, false accusers, incontinent, fierce, and despisers of those that are good. They will be traitors, heady, high-minded lovers of pleasure *more than* lovers of God. {Romans 1:29-31}. As the days of Noah were before the flood, when people were going about their daily lives as always—sinning and being sinned against—until the flood came and took them away; so the coming of the Son of Man shall be! {Matthew 24:30, Luke 17:26-30}.

As the lightening comes out of the east and shines even into the west, so shall Christ's second coming be. When *that* day comes, the arrogance of the proud will cease, and the haughtiness of the terrible will be laid low! For who can abide the day of his coming, and who shall stand when *He* appears? All their wealth will not be able to save them on that day, for the whole land will be devoured by the fire of God's fierce jealousy! {Zephaniah 1:18}.

The Lord Jesus Christ is like a refiner's fire, and he and his mighty angels in flaming fire shall take vengeance on those who know not God and that do not hear his gospel. The scriptures say "Woe unto you that desire the pending doom that will be brought forth on the dreadful day of the Lord (which will come as a thief in the night) for the day of the Lord is gloom and thick darkness—it is *not* light! It is a day of wrath, trouble, distress, barren waste, and desolation! It brings forth the wrath and fierce anger of God upon all nations, and even the mighty men will cry bitterly. And it says "Woe to them that are with child, because in those days there will be such a cry and such tribulation, such as there has not been since the beginning of the world to this time." The proud and the wicked will have their blood poured out as dust, their flesh as dung, and they shall be burnt into stubble! They shall be punished with everlasting destruction from the presence of the Lord and from the glory of his power. On that dreadful day, the powers of heaven shall be shaken...

The sun will be darkened!
The moon will not give her light!
The stars will fall from heaven!
The heavens themselves shall be dissolved and pass away
with a great noise!
The elements will melt with fervent heat!
The earth and its works shall be burned up!

{Joel 2:10, 31, 3:14-15, Matthew 24:29-30, Mark 13:24-26, Luke 21:25-27, Acts 2:20, Revelation 6:16-17}.

Who can take these statements of Holy Scripture lightly? No one in their right mind! When the Lord of Hosts leaves the wicked neither root nor branch, and except those days be shortened, there would be no flesh saved at all...and the human race would cease to exist. {Matthew 24:21-22}.

God Answers His Critics

HE who places flaming swords at the guideposts to Life Eternal—HIS words are sharper than any two-edged sword! What right has anyone to question this One and Only Almighty Omnipotent God? For it is from out of the whirlwind that HE answers his critics and asks "Have you not heard, have you not understood...?"

And HE speaks...

"Let it be known that My anger is revealed from heaven against all the sin and evil of those whose evil ways prevent the truth from being known. I punish them, because what can be known about Me is plain to them, for I myself made it plain. Ever since I created the world, my invisible qualities, both My eternal power and divine nature, have been clearly seen; they are perceived in the things that I have made. So the so-called "atheist" has no excuse at all! They know Me, but they do not give Me the honor that belongs to Me, nor do they thank Me. Instead, their thoughts have become complete nonsense, and their empty minds are filled with darkness. They say they are wise, but they are fools. They exchange the truth about Me for a lie, and instead of worshipping their Immortal Creator, they worship and serve those perishable things that He has created, such as *mortal* man, or birds, or animals, or reptiles. And so I have given them over to do the filthy things their hearts desire, and to dishonor their own bodies between themselves. Men give up natural sexual relations with women and burn with passion for each other. They do shameful things with each other, and as a result they bring upon themselves the punishment they deserve for their wrongdoing. Even the women pervert the natural use of their sex through their vile affections.

Because these people refuse to retain Me in their knowledge, I have given them over to a reprobate mind. Being without understanding, they are filled with all unrighteousness. But I tell you the day is coming when I will render to every man according to his deeds. To them who by patient continuance in well doing seek for glory and honor and immortality, *eternal life.* But unto them that are contentious, and do not obey the truth, but choose to obey unrighteousness, *indignation and wrath.* These people know that My Law says that people who live in this way deserve death. Yet not only do they continue to do these very things, but they also even approve of others who do them. To the disobedient and unclean, even when they pray they pray in vain because what they ask for in prayer they ask for according to their desires of the flesh.

Even your words have been stout against Me...You have said it is vain to serve God for what profit is it to keep his laws and walk mournfully before him? And now you call the proud happy; and say that those who work wickedness are lifted up, even those who *tempt* God.

You are departed out of the way; you have caused many to stumble at the law. Therefore have I also made you contemptible and base before all the people, according to your rejection of My ways and your partiality in the law.

Cursed be the deceiver for...I am a great King saith the Lord of Hosts, and My name is dreadful among the heathen. I am the Lord, I change not."

{Romans 1:18-32, James 4:3, Malachi 1:14, 2:8-9, 3:6, 3:13-15}.

Yes, the unrepentant, disobedient willful violators of God's Laws are going to have to gird up their loins and give an account for their deeds to their Creator. The wisdom of this world is but foolishness in *His* sight. Yes, He who is and was and is to come is no respecter of man, and he has *warned* us not to follow the wisdom of this world.

A Suffering World: Not From God

God's desire is to give mercy, not revenge. It is not his wish that *any* should perish, but that *all* should come to repentance. Convincing people that God either does not exist or that he could care less about humanity and all its problems, Satan leads many to say "If God does exist, then *why* does He permit suffering?" But truth from error does not change with God. The wicked and violent world we live in and the suffering that we see does *not* come from God. It comes from our own choices, for God does not put man to the test through temptations, *Satan* does! God would never do anything that would cause man's separation *from* Him. As we have seen, God condemns evil acts. Did He not declare this in the very laws he gave to man through his servant Moses?

If we reject God long enough, is it not justice for him to reject *us*? If we abandon God from our daily lives, he will (at some point) remove the restraints of his loving and saving grace, and he will give us over to our own desires. Shall we then cry out against Him when we experience the results of our very own choices? When overcome by grief or sorrow, will we say "How could *God* allow *this* to happen?

Of course there are those who will say, "If God is a loving god, then why did he create the devil in the first place?" And to this I would once again ask *who are we to judge God?* As we have seen, God did not create the devil, he created an angel of incredible beauty. And that angel, possessing free moral agency (like all of God's creatures) *chose* self-pride over God's laws. And thus he fell from grace. God could have destroyed that fallen angel Lucifer at the moment of his sin. But had God done so, as all the other angels looked on, the question of sin versus God's Law would have remained unanswered. And then should God have gone through all eternity destroying the curious of his creation at the very moment of their curiosity? No. God is not a maker of mindless robots. He chose to give all free will. It is His desire to let man come to him out of love, respect, and *choice*. And so He has chosen to let man, like the angels, find out for himself which is the better way to live.

The Results Of Our Own Choices

In today's modern world, we say we have progressed. We believe we live in an era of high technology. We say "See this? See that? Just look at all the things *we* have created. We do not need God; we are self-sufficient."

In our self-derived wisdom, we have even sent rocket probes into outer space. NASA's stated goal is to find life on other planets. They spend billions of dollars in an attempt to prove that life evolved by natural processes, instead of being created by the supernatural powers of God. When they recently studied the pictures that a probe on Mars sent back to earth, scientists said that they had found evidence of a "global flood" on Mars. They based their conclusions on the evidence of what appear to be erosional gullies. "If there was once water on Mars, there must have been life, because water sustains life." they claim. But in all their hoopla and *hope*la, they disregard the fact that right here, on a planet that is *currently* two-thirds covered by water, that a global flood did occur—the evidence overwhelmingly supports it! But they reject that idea because it brings to mind the thought that the Bible could actually be true!

Not only has NASA poured out extreme amounts of money (that could be used for the improvement of mankind right here on *this* planet), but they also have the backing of our illustrious leaders in Washington to do so. The president and vice-president not only back it, but they also hope to see the finding of evidence of life on another planet come to fruition. As vice-president Al Gore said recently regarding the photos from Mars, "Perhaps the evidence found there will shed light on our own evolution."

Instead of improving life on this planet, we are eliminating it. In all of our wisdom, we have now devised the means by which we kill the youngest members of humanity, the defenseless *brephos*, and we say that it's okay to do so—that it is within the law! But whose law? Not God's law. What was once sacred and protected in its mother's womb, is now helpless prey to so-called "medical professionals" who mercilessly hack it to pieces or burn it to death with an acidic solution. Is *this* what we call progress?

In all of our wisdom, we are starting to put an end to the lives of our sick and elderly by killing them with lethal injections, and we are calling it "mercy."

In all of our wisdom, we have devised the means by which we can utterly destroy ourselves with weapons of mass destruction. Is *this* progress too?

In all of our wisdom, we have declared that a woman's value is somehow lessened if she doesn't place more emphasis on a career than on the rearing of her own children.

And now, in all of our wisdom, we have begun to use the technology of television and radio to convince people that the gay lifestyle should be accepted as normal; that it's something to be proud of.

I think it's time our leaders get off their high horses and get back to the basics. As history has proven, it does not belong to man to direct his own footsteps independent of God. As Henry Morris would put it "It's time to get back to Genesis."

Enduring Trials and Tribulations

Some men come in God's name. They profess to know Him with their words, but their *deeds* tell a different story. Because of them, many turn away from God. Because of them, many even blame God for terrible religious wars such as the Crusades and the inquisitions. Because of them, many blame God for modern day terrorist activities. But God does not approve of workers of lawlessness or iniquity even if they *believe* what they are doing is right. Their sincere belief in what they do is of little value to God, for he gave them a code of conduct to live by, and they have refused to adhere to it.

It is in their own choices to live independent of Him, that many have found confusion, unhappiness, suffering, sickness, and even death. They choose to follow the ways of envy, pride, arrogance, stubbornness, deceitfulness, gossip, hatred, lust, and self-love instead...all of which are attributes of Satan, the devil.

It's Not God's Will For People To Be Sorrowful

If we begin to complain during our trials and tribulations, it will help us to understand that if we live according to His will, God can turn every set-back, every adversity, every heartache, and even every tragedy into the seed of a greater benefit, for God is a worker of miracles.

It is through trials that man learns to have greater appreciation. It is through tribulation that man is strengthened to overcome personal weaknesses. It is through trials and tribulations that man either grows in faith or allows his heart to be hardened against God. It is through these very things that man is separated onto two distinctively different paths; one leading to salvation, the other to destruction!

If we look to Jesus as the pattern to follow, have we any right to complain during these times in our lives? For it was through his obedience to God the Father, that Jesus endured *ultimate suffering* on *our* behalf. He was made perfect through his obedience and sufferings. As a result, His name was lifted above every other name. Through his obedience to God the Father, Jesus has been given ultimate power and authority. Should we not therefore strive to be as he taught us to be?

The Bottom Line

What is the bottom line regarding men having sexual relationships with men, or women having sexual relationships with women (referred to in the King James Version of the Holy Bible as *lying with*)? In other words, what is the bottom line regarding homosexuality? God has stated in his word, not only that which you have already read, but also the following:

In Genesis 19:4-7 we read of how the men of Sodom surrounded Lot's house and *demanded* that he turn the two men who were visiting him over to them so that they could "know" them. Lot replied "I pray you bretheren, do not do so wickedly."

In Leviticus 18:22 God, in speaking to man, said "Thou shalt not lie with mankind as with womankind; it *is* abomination."

In Leviticus 20:13 "If a man lie with mankind as he lieth with a woman, both of them have committed an abomination; they shall surely be put to death; their blood shall be upon them."

In Deuteronomy 22:5 "The woman shall not wear that which pertaineth unto a man, neither shall a man put on a woman's garment: for all that do so *are* abomination unto the Lord thy God.

Psalm 7:11-13 tells us that "God judges the righteous, and God is angry with the wicked every day. If he turn not, he will whet his sword; he has bent his bow, and made it ready. He has also prepared for him the instruments of death; he ordains his arrows against the persecutors."

In both Matthew 19:4-6 and Mark 10:6-9 Christ himself reaffirms the teaching of Genesis 1:27 and 2:24 where God laid out the foundational design of acceptable behavior for human sexuality. Jesus said "From the beginning of creation God made them male and female. For this cause shall a man leave his father and mother and cleave to his wife. And they twain shall be one flesh, so then they are no more twain, but one flesh. What therefore God hath joined together, let not man put asunder.

1st Corinthians 6:9-11 tells us not to be deceived: that those who continue to be *effeminate* will not inherit the Kingdom of God.

1st Corinthians 6:18 tells us to flee fornication for it is a sin against our own bodies.

1st Thessalonians 4:3-6 tells us that it is God's will that we be sanctified, that we abstain from fornication, that we learn to control our bodies, that no man go beyond and defraud his brother in *any* manner, and that we learn to live a holy and honorable life.

1st Timothy 1:8-10 tells us that the law was not made for the righteous man, but for the disobedient and for those who defile themselves with one another.

And finally, Jude 5-7 says "Remember how the Lord, having saved the people out of the land of Egypt, afterward destroyed them that believed not. And the angels which kept not their first estate, but left their own habitation, he hath reserved in everlasting chains under darkness unto the judgment of the great day. Even as Sodom and Gomorrah, and the cities about them in like manner, giving themselves over to fornication, and *going after strange flesh*, are set forth for and example (as a plain warning to all) suffering the vengeance of eternal fire."

How much more plain can the Bible be regarding this issue of homosexuality? So let us hear the bottom line concerning this matter: If you are living the gay lifestyle and do not repent, then you are living *in* sin and *against* Almighty God. And as you have seen, the Lord God is great and all-powerful—He is to be highly praised, and humbly feared!

God has promised us that if we walk in the spirit, we will not fulfill the lust of the flesh. He has also said those who humble themselves as little children are like those who are the greatest in heaven. Having therefore heard these promises, let us cleanse ourselves from all filthiness of the flesh and of the spirit, obey his commandments, and strive for the perfection of holiness that can only come by first having a healthy fear of God, for this is the whole duty of man.

Chapter Five

GOD'S MERCY REVEALED

Through Christ

Blessed be the God and Father of our Lord Jesus Christ, which according to his abundant mercy has begotten us again into a lively hope by the resurrection of Jesus Christ from the dead.

I KNOW OF A WOMAN WHO HAD A GOOD FAMILY life. But that woman had an affair with her boss at work, left her husband, and broke up her family. When her little girl asked her why she was leaving daddy, she explained that "sometimes people fall out of love." How sad and tragic this story is, but one that is becoming more and more typical in our society today. Now I don't hate this woman, I hate the sin that caused her to go astray. Perhaps that same woman, and others like her, would point the proverbial finger at the author because he too has sinned in the past, as have we all. But I have since repented of those sins. I am truly sorrowful for the things I did when I was engulfed by sin. I now rest upon God's mercy through the shed blood of Christ as my only hope for salvation. When you bring it all down, isn't that all *any* of us can hope for?

I did not come through the pages of this book to pass judgment on others for they have enough of their own problems, as do we all. No, I will not point the proverbial finger at others in order that I may look down my nose at them and attempt to relieve any of the guilt resulting from my own sinful past. And no, this author does not hate Ellen DeGeneres or Oprah Winfrey or anyone else for that matter. I do hate, however, the sin that some stand up for, and that *is* sexual immorality. Some have promoted this sinful lifestyle not only to the adults of our nation, but to our children as well. And this I speak out against, and I speak for many.

I came here to speak the truth. By shedding light on the truth of this matter, I hope that the pages written herein will turn people to God. By bearing witness to the truth, if He is willing, these words will help to change the minds of those who are either intentionally living in rejection of His Laws, or those who have been deceived by the media.

There are those who hate sinners and at the same time believe themselves to be Christians. As for those who hate the sinner instead of the sin, may I remind you that the Scriptures tell us to be merciful, for God is merciful to us. They also tell us that by the same measure by which we judge others, we too will be judged. The message is clear: Condemn not and you shall not be condemned! And so we are instructed to forgive, and we shall be forgiven; to *love* our enemies and to *pray for them,* for far worse is their plight than anything we could ever wish upon them, even in our weakest, most scornful moments.

Passing judgment on sinners is Christ's job. He is much better equipped to handle that, for only he knows all the factors involved. But I do believe that the followers of Christ have a duty to expose sin for what it *really* is. The *Oprah Winfrey* and *Ellen* shows that promoted the acceptance of the gay lifestyle awakened a spirit in the Christian community. And the Spirit said "Look, they are deceiving people!"

The New Covenant
As we travel through God's word as found in the Holy Bible, we find that around eighty percent of the Scriptures are Old

Testament writings. Only around twenty percent are New Testament. If we do an overview of the summaries of the books of the Old Testament, we see a recurring theme throughout history. That theme is that people who have been blessed by God become discouraged when they haven't heard from him in a while. Their discouragement leads to rebellion, which in turn leads to the removal of God's blessings. Then it becomes "open season" for humanity, and Satan and his followers go hunting! It is important to note however, that *even during times of human rebellion,* God often remained patient and still provided for his people in spite of their disobedience to his laws.

When we come to the New Testament, things change. The theme is no longer one of blessing then cursing, then blessing then cursing again, but it becomes centered around the life of Jesus Christ instead. Perhaps one of the reasons for the change is because the Lord was no longer in heaven blessing then cursing, but was instead walking among us! In any case, God declared in his word that he made a new covenant with man in which he stated that he would be merciful—even to man's unrighteousness.

It is God's will for men to be reconciled unto himself. By creating a new covenant with man, God showed that he is patient, long-suffering, and kind to man so that those who repent and strive to live honestly and obey him, will in the end be made perfect in every good work through Jesus Christ, and therefore become pleasing in God's sight. And Jesus, being the mediator of the better covenant which was established upon better promises, became the offering that paid the price for guilty man because all sin is (by the law of God) purged with blood. Without the shedding of blood, there is no remission. So Christ was offered up to bear the sins of many. Unto them that look for Him shall he appear the second time as the author of eternal salvation; unto them who do not—the eternal judgment.

Christ *Is* The Arrow

Jesus Christ is the arrow that points to the one true path of everlasting happiness! Years ago, the title for this book came to the author's mind as one that sounded good, but the subject matter originally planned for the book was going to center around the authenticity and inerrancy of the Bible. The book originally set out to shed light on the teaching of false doctrines, such as evolution, but the title didn't fit the subject matter. That was *until* the Oprah and *Ellen* shows. Those shows changed the direction of the book, and the title—like a bolt from the blue—struck once again, and this time it fit its subject matter perfectly and *to the word*. So the author grabbed a dictionary and looked up the meanings of each word in the title, and here's what he found:

<u>As</u>:
1) to such a degree or extent...*that it is.*
<u>Straight</u>:
1) without bend, angle, or curve; it is exactly vertical or
      horizontal...*not twisted, as by false doctrines.*
2) honest or frank...*the Bible is both.*
3) right or correct, as thinking...*unlike human philosophies.*
4) in the proper order or condition...*all things occur in their due
      time, according to the will of God.*
5) continuous or unbroken...*as chains of events are in the Bible.*
6) undiluted or unmixed...*as by opinions.*
7) normal or conventional, heterosexual...*normal indicates the
      fact that deviance from it can be nothing but <u>abnormal</u>.*
<u>As</u>:
2) as is; just the way it appears or exists...*Christ embodies truth;
      the Bible is factual, and both separate truth from error.*
<u>An</u>:
1) a suffix meaning of or belonging to...*Jesus belonged to God
      way before he ever became a man.*
<u>Arrow</u>:
1) a figure that indicates direction...*direction derived from the
      Bible and Jesus Christ himself.*
2) a slender, pointed missile equipped with feathers at the end
      of the shaft, shot from a bow...*although it is thin and light-
      weight, an arrow packs incredible force when it is shot or
      propelled toward a target. The humble Christ's words have
      done the same, and they continue to do so to this very day!*

An arrow is only as good as the hand of the archer! It takes great strength for an archer to be able to shoot straight and be good at hitting his mark. That strength is derived from patience, skill, and practice. Jesus, who was in the hand of God the Father himself, was as the arrow that is guided by the Master Archer. His strength (spiritual, mental, and emotional) was gained through his longstanding and loving relationship with his Father, and he has related that strength to his followers. And many followers he has had an impact on, indeed. One who comes to mind is Sir Isaac Newton, who was voted to be the greatest contributor to science (of all time) by the scientific community. Newton said this:

"The book of Revelation exhibits to us the same peculiarities as that of Nature...The history of the Fall of Man—of the introduction of moral and physical evil, the prediction of the Messiah, the actual advent of our Savior, His instructions, His miracles, His death, His resurrection, and the subsequent propagation of His religion by the unlettered fishermen of Galilee, are each a stumbling-block to the wisdom of this world...But through the system of revealed truth which this Book contains is, like that of the universe, concealed from common observation, yet the labors of the centuries have established its Divine origin, and developed in all its order and beauty the great plan of human restoration."

Ah yes, can it be true that the greatest scientist who ever lived was a Bible-believing Christian? "This I know, (said the author unknown) that Jesus Christ opens hearts by opening minds."

When They Crucified The Lord

Where were *you* when they crucified our Lord? We all crucified him you know. Yes, we all crucified the spotless, blameless Lamb of God; the altogether lovely one who was like the beautiful flower that gave off a pleasing fragrance when it was stepped on!

Something to think about, isn't it? The man who was more

holy than Mohammed, more holy than Buddha, more holy than Noah or Moses or Joshua or Abraham or any high priest or monk or evangelist who ever walked the face of the earth was... betrayed by one of his followers, arrested, and made to stand before a mock trial. After the church leaders falsely accused him, one of his closest friends denied even knowing him! He was then bound and handed over to the governmental authorities. A mob gathered, and the governor offered them the freedom of one of two prisoners; Jesus, or a man named Barabbas (who was a murderer and a thief).

The crowd chose Barabbas.

The incited crowd then insisted upon the crucifixion of Jesus! So to appease the mob, the powers that be took Jesus and stripped him naked. To shame him, they made him wear a scarlet robe and a painful crown of thorns. He was then ridiculed, made fun of, slapped, blindfolded, beat over the head with a stick, and spat upon! His hide was lashed into with a cat-o'-nine-tails, and then the Roman soldiers made him carry a heavy wooden cross through the streets of the city. When they got outside the city walls and had reached the place of the skull known as Golgotha (in Aramaic) also known as Calvary (in Latin), they laid him down on a wooden cross and drove spikes through his hands and feet into the cross.

While he hung there to that cross in excruciating pain, blood dripped from his forehead, it dripped from his back, it dripped from his hands, and it dripped from his feet. Drip, drip, drip went the blood down the cross and onto the ground. His ligaments slowly began to tear, causing him to slowly and painfully suffocate. And each time he would try to pull himself up to catch a breath and avoid the tearing of his muscles, his lashed and bloody back would rub against the wooden beam... causing even more pain.

And while all this was taking place, what were the people of the world doing? They were eating and drinking, and going about business as usual. The Roman soldiers were dividing his clothes among themselves. They even rolled dice to see who would get which piece of his clothing! The people passing by shook their heads and hurled insults at him... And thus he had become the epitome of shame to a sinning, greedy, and unforgiving world—*our* unforgiving world that is.

For three agonizing hours...drip, drip, drip went the blood. It poured out of his vessel to the very world that scorned him. And yet in spite of all of his pain, and in spite of all of our wickedness toward him, Jesus prayed to his Father...

"Forgive them, for they know not what they do." {Luke 23:34}.

The Scriptures tell us that during his earthly ministry when Jesus would pray, he always prayed using the word "Father." But when he hung there on that cross, and the bitter anguish and agony of his nearing death fell upon him, and the sin of the world fell upon him, and the wrath of God fell upon him *for our sakes*, he could endure no more, and he cried out "My God, My God, Why hast thou forsaken me?" {Matthew 27:46}. It was only during this period of bearing the heavy burden of sin, that Jesus had to be detached from his Father, and he called out to him as "God" instead of "Father."

No Cheap Grace

Jesus not only withstood the torture of man, but he also bore all the sins man has or ever will commit. He drank the bitter cup of indignation that was filled with all manner of vile affections...for our sakes. He drank the cup that we deserved in order that we may be saved. And finally, when the whole nightmare was over, he cried out loud... "Father, into thy hands I commend my spirit." And then he died. {Luke 23:46}. And just to make sure he was dead, a Roman soldier plunged a spear into his side, and at once blood and water gushed out. {John 19:34}.

Today, many people will put on a nice pair of clothes and go to church on Sunday. Once there, they will sing some hymns, listen to a sermon, and maybe even say some prayers. Then when Church is over, they will go back home and relax for a day. Then when the workweek starts they will once again begin to live a life of sin...from Monday through Saturday! If they are ever asked if they believe in Christ, they reply "Yes. I even go to church on Sunday."

You see, they believe in cheap grace. They may not call it that, but that is what their conduct reveals. The apostle Paul warned the members of the Church at Rome of this very thing when he said "...Shall we continue in sin, that grace may abound? God forbid. How shall we, that are dead to sin, live any longer therein?" {Romans 6:1-2}.

Yes, God is long suffering. Yes, His love endures. And yes, His mercy is a gift that is offered freely. *But His grace is no cheap grace!* It did not come without a price. As you have already seen, God is a god of love, but he's also a god of justice. And His justice demands that a penalty be paid for sin. And He himself took care of the penalty of our sins for us through his very own son!

Yes, we all crucified the very Son of God! Some of us betrayed him, some of us abandoned him, some of us tortured him, and some of us murdered him. Some of us have repented of those terrible deeds. Others have not. Some still willfully continue to crucify him and reject his name. As a result, they unknowingly have tossed aside His rich mercy (and subsequently their own salvation) and they are still under the wrath of God.

Mercy Available To All

Out of His love for humanity, God the Father sent his son (his *only* son) to earth. He did not send him here to die for nothing. There was (and is) a great cause: a *universal cause*. All those long list of names in the Bible that provide us with the genealogy of important figures, especially Christ, shows that God knows each and every person by name. He knows all of us on a very personal level. We are not like some tiny little ants that are scurrying around beneath the notice of an angry giant God. No, the Creator is far more caring. He created each of us in the very image of Himself, and he did so through his only begotten Son. He sees us as potential members of His very own family. This is not vague wishful thinking on the part of the author, it is a statement of fact based upon the word of God as found in the Holy Scriptures.

With God All Things Are Possible

Some believe they are inadequate to be saved and become members of the God family. They feel that their sin has alienated them from God to the extent that the gap to be bridged is too wide—it's just too far for them to be brought back to righteousness. But let me reassure you of one very important fact, and that is this: every single person living today has erred, blundered, messed up, fouled up, screwed up, made BIG mistakes, etc. In short, every one of us has sinned! And we know what the punishment for sin is. But as Psalm 118 tells us *five times*, God's mercy "endureth forever." Let us not forget that this is the One and Only God we're talking about here. It is He that stretched out the heavens as a curtain, and spread them out as a tent to dwell in. It is He that spoke the very light that we see by into existence. This is the One who stretched out his hand and created the heavens and the earth. To Him, the nations are as a drop of a bucket, and are counted as the small dust of the balance. So to whom then will we liken Him? In what likeness will we compare Him to? With whom did He take counsel when he created theses things? Who taught Him in the ways of knowledge, understanding, and righteousness?

What we're talking about here folks, is a Mighty and Omnipotent God, not an impotent one! Our God is a capable God—he can help to solve *any* problem. Knowing this, why should anyone feel so unique that condemnation (for him or her) is eminent? *It is not!* If they will simply lift up their eyes on high and behold who has created these things, then day by day they will come to know that God *is* God. That fact alone should make them turn their life around. That's what happened to Amy Tracy.

Nobody's Perfect

Amy Tracy worked as the president of the Alexandria, Va., chapter of the National Organization for Woman (NOW). She worked for their national office in Washington, D.C., serving as press secretary where she battled on the front lines for both abortion and gay rights. She also had an intimate three-year affair with another woman. But that was all *before* she came to realize the truth.

"I believed I had ultimate freedom to act, speak, and believe as I wanted, and to choose whom I loved. This "freedom" however, eventually enslaved me." she said. For nearly three years, Tracy was prompted by God to change her way of life, but she refused. "Part of my confusion stemmed from the fact that I could not reconcile my heart's yearning (to know Christ) with the hostile behavior I encountered in some Christians. Rarely did I see anyone reflecting the heart or nature of the God pursuing me." God did not give up on her however, and after a three-year battle with inner turmoil, Tracy said she "could no longer ignore the absence of absolute truth in the mind-set of the gay community." In September 1995, Amy Tracy accepted an invitation from God to accept Christ as her Savior, and she abandoned her former way of life.

Ron Elmore was once steeped knee-deep in the homosexual lifestyle as well. He had lived a painful past of both abandonment (he was placed in an orphanage at an early age) and of sexual abuse (he was molested—not only by a family friend, but also by some older boys and even some authoritative figures). He let his painful past push him into even more pain, and he began to abuse alcohol, drugs, and pornography. But somewhere along the way, Elmore was compelled to look into the Bible, and *there* he found the words that eventually led to his deliverance from those addictions, from the homosexuality, and from the pain he felt from his dreary past. He now has a wife, and he heads up a ministry to those struggling with sexual addictions.

John Paulk is another example of God's grace. Paulk's parents divorced when he was just little. The insecurity he felt from his parents' break-up showed up in his relationships with other boys. Because he lacked masculinity, he was picked on and he began drinking in his early teen years to "ease the pain." While he was still in high school, his search for acceptance led him into a gay bar. He found acceptance, but he embraced the gay lifestyle to do so. And embrace it he did—with all the trimmings. Alcohol addiction, drug abuse, and male prostitution all reared their ugly heads in Paulk's life as he struggled with this sin. He even became a well-known female impersonator (drag queen), and eventually attempted suicide to rid himself of all his pain. But *God* had different plans for John Paulk. One day a college pastor pointed out a scripture passage to John—and his eyes were opened!

It took several years, but Paulk too has now "returned to his first estate." By embracing Christ, his lifestyle went from negative (and dangerous), to positive (and healthy). By God's grace, John had been saved from the homosexual lifestyle. Now, through God's divine providence, John is married to a woman from his church named Anne, and they have something in common. You see, she too had struggled in her past—with lesbianism!

John and Anne Paulk have spoken publicly regarding their struggles with the gay lifestyle...and the renewed happiness they found through the transforming power of Jesus Christ. The couple has been married now for seven years and have two sons. John has written a book on the subject of his life entitled *Not Afraid to Change*, and both he and his wife have written a book together entitled *Love Won Out*.

Eric Harrah is another person who walked away from homosexuality. But that's not all. You see, Eric spent a decade in the abortion trade. He openly referred to himself as a "baby killer." As part owner or operator of some twenty-six abortion clinics that provided an estimated 250,000 abortions during his tenure, Eric Harrah (a big man who had an even bigger temper) was a force to be reckoned with. He even advertised his services with the phone number 1-800-ABORTION!

But Eric Harrah, as bad as he *was*, was no match for the conversion power of Jesus Christ, who sent another big man (with an even bigger heart) named Steve Stupar, to help Eric. Through persistence, prayer, and unconditional friendship, Stupar became the vessel that God used to shake loose the shackles of Harrah's bondage to sin. As a result, Eric Harrah accepted Jesus Christ as his personal lord and savior, and walked away from not only the abortion trade and the wealth he had derived from it, but from the homosexual lifestyle as well.

These are but a few examples of people who have chosen to turn their lives around. They have found freedom from sexual sin through the mercy of Jesus Christ. Thousands of other individuals have left the gay lifestyle behind as well. Their testimonials provide the best examples of *hope* that can be found anywhere.

Acceptance *Is* Enough

If you've committed acts of homosexuality, you too can still be saved, because Christ said he will save *anyone* who comes unto him and believes upon him. What the law of the Old Testament could not do, in that it was weak through the flesh, God sending his own son in the likeness of sinful flesh, and *for* sin, condemned sin in the flesh. So no matter what the sin may be, the *person* can be saved if he or she comes to Christ because he became sin (all sin) for us. All sin is covered by His atoning blood.

Earlier you read that when it comes to the items that are outlined in the gay rights agenda, that acceptance is not enough. Well what we are talking about here (accepting Christ) *is* enough. If you are living in the turmoil of the gay lifestyle, you don't have to accept a message of "tolerance" based upon false hopes. You don't have to explain to anyone about the decisions that you have made to this point. You don't even have to try to win an argument with a so-called "right wing extremist." All you have to do is accept Jesus Christ at his word. That's all.

What we're talking about here folks is a message of LIFE. It's about *eternal salvation!* Once you accept the gift of grace that God has offered freely, then your lifestyle *will* change. And although the road to freedom from the gay lifestyle is seldom a smoothly paved one, it is nevertheless an *available* one. It is available to those who throw their struggles, their fears, and their hopes upon Christ. And when *that* happens, there is no condemnation, but only love and acceptance. People can let other people down—that's a fact of life—even within the churches. But Jesus *is* different. It is Jesus who remains committed to the offer of hope and healing... for he and he alone stands ready. He provides dispensation of grace.

Paul's Example

God will quicken those who at one time walked according to their lust of the flesh if they hear his words and obey. Take the apostle Paul, for example. Before his conversion to Christianity, Paul, originally named Saul, was a terrible sinner who, among other things, blasphemed against God and hated and zealously imprisoned and persecuted Christians! And yet during his lifetime he became the writer of at least thirteen of the twenty-seven books of the New Testament! In the first epistle he wrote to the Corinthians, Paul posed a question that if answered honestly would convict most people of their sexual sins. He said this: "Know ye not that you are the temple of God, and that the Spirit of God dwelleth in you? If any man defile the temple of God, him shall God destroy; for the temple of God is holy, which temple ye are." {1Corinthians 3:16-17}.

If Christ is willing not only to save, but also to make an apostle out of a man who was so antagonistic to his followers, how much more can he do for those who are merely lost in sexual sin? The Bible states that He is able to do *exceeding abundantly above* all that we ask or think. {Ephesians 3:20}.

The Hand That Faileth Not

In the Old Testament, God told his prophet, Ezekiel, to write these words: "Neither shall they defile themselves any more with their idols, nor with their detestable things, nor with any of their transgressions: but I will save them out of all their dwelling places, wherein they have sinned, and will cleanse them: so they shall be my people, and I will be their God." {Ezekiel 37:23}.

In the days of old, God told his people *"Return unto me, and I will return unto you."* He told them that if they lived according to his laws, and obeyed his commands, that he would send them rain at the right time so that their land would produce crops and the trees would bear fruit.

Have your "trees" bore good fruit? They can. Indeed, God's rich mercy is available to all of us who are willing to go forth and sin no more. As we have seen, He has proven that he will deliver those who come to Christ and sincerely give their lives over to him. God does not say in his word that those who were at one time living the gay lifestyle will not inherit the Kingdom, but those who *are* will not.

To sum it all up, any one who repents of their sin has an advocate with the Father...in Jesus. Jesus Christ, the righteous, *is* the propitiation for our sins, and we know that we know him, if we keep his commandments. The Bible cannot be more plain on this subject than when it indefatigably states: "For the wages of sin *is* death: but the gift of God *is* eternal life through Jesus Christ our Lord" {Romans 6:23}.

Chapter Six

OVERCOMING TEMPTATION

Through The Armour

ACCORDING TO HIS DIVINE POWER, GOD GIVES TO
us all things that pertain to life and godliness through abundant
knowledge of himself. He has called us to glory and virtue. He
has given great promises of unimaginable joy in the world to
come to those who endure the trials of this life, and escape the
corruption that is in this world.

Called To Virtue

As we have seen, we are explicitly told in the Bible that we are
to abstain from fornication and all other immoral sexual
practices. We are to know how to possess our vessels in
sanctification and honor, for God has not called us unto

uncleanness, but unto *holiness!* Jesus even told us that if our hand or foot offends us, that we should cut them off and cast them away from us. And He told us that if our eye offends us, that we should pluck it out and cast it away as well. He said these things to show us that it is better to enter into life maimed, than to be cast into eternal fire with all our members. {Matthew 5:29-30, 18:8-9}. Whether he was speaking symbolically or not, we get the point!

Dr. Michael Misja, Co-founder and Director of the Northcoast Family Foundation, and radio host of *The Dr. Michael Show,* has said that Christians are better off expressing *what they stand for,* as opposed to *why they are against* the gay lifestyle. For example, he said...

"We are for:
  *The joy that only monogamy can bring to a man and wife.
  *The freedom of conscience a person committed to a
    monogamous lifestyle enjoys.
  *The freedom from disease a person who practices abstinence
    has.
  *The security parents and children enjoy when parents are
    faithful to one another.
  *The delight God knows when his children celebrate their
    commitment to each other."

Dr. Michael says "It's not just about sex. It's about integrity, discipline, morality, and submission to the wisdom of the God of the Universe."

Yes, in His Word, God has instructed us that we are to diligently add to our faith virtue, and to that virtue knowledge, and to knowledge temperance, and to temperance patience, and to patience godliness, and to godliness brotherly kindness, and to brotherly kindness charity. {2Peter 1:3-7}. We are told that we should not strive to please ourselves (as most do today) but to please our neighbors; to build *them* up in faith to follow the example set forth by Christ. We are told to guard our hearts, put away perverse lips, keep our eyes set on good things, and ponder the path of our feet.{Proverbs 4:21-26}. In other words, we have been called to *virtue.*

But one may be inclined to ask how we can do these things with all the pressures we face. And the answer is that we obtain a virtuous character *gradually* by submitting our minds and bodies to the will of God, and by resisting the devil. And although we will grow stronger with each resistance of sin, we still need to put on the full armour of God.

The Way To Escape Sexual Sin

The way to escape sexual sin (or any other sin for that matter) is described in the Bible as "putting on the whole Armour of God." {Ephesians 6:11}. It is *not* found by frequenting gay bars! The Bible tells us that in order to overcome our weaknesses through those things which tempt us... that we are to walk in the day, be sober, be vigilant, and avoid rioting, drunkenness, indecency, wantonness, strife, and envy. We are to make no provision to fulfill the lust of the flesh because our adversary, the devil, is roaming around seeking whomever he can to devour!

The Bible also tells us that God will not *let* us be tempted beyond that which we can bear. As we have seen, temptations to sin do not come from God, but from Satan. As a matter of fact, it is God who gives us the strength to endure trials. It is He who provides us with a way out—even if it must be *through* the trials that we must travel in order to be strengthened! This is how God purges, cleanses, and refines us. He tells us to resist the devil, and in so doing, the devil will flee from us. {James 4:7}.

So it is by submitting ourselves to God, that we weak human beings can resist the powerful devil. When we submit ourselves to God, he gives us the knowledge we need to protect ourselves from the wiles of Satan, for the devil has a distinct advantage over those who are *unaware* of his tactics. You see, ignorance, when it comes to dealing with the powerful beguiling serpent is not bliss; it is *dangerous.* It is like the young child that has watched his father pour lighter fluid on the logs and then light the match to start a campfire in order to cook the food. But then on a different day, the young child (in ignorance) tries to do the same thing with the *grill* that his father has lit...after the father has went inside to get some plates! And when the child pours the fluid on the already lighted grill, the flame travels up the stream of lighter fluid to the can—which is in the young child's hand—and it explodes in his face! It is a tragedy that could have been avoided if it were not for *lack of knowledge.*

The more knowledge we have of the devil's schemes, the more chance we have of overcoming those temptations that he sends our way. In 2 Corinthians 2:11 it says "Lest Satan should get an advantage of us, for we are not ignorant of his devices." But within the gaining of knowledge, there also lies warnings. We have to be careful that the knowledge we gain does not "puff us up." The Bible warns against this, and it says it is better to love one's neighbor than to be full of pride gained from knowledge. We also have to be careful not to gain our knowledge by studying or dwelling on the devil or his devices such as common place astrology, psychic channeling, necromancy, hydromancy, rhabdomancy, witchcraft or any other divination method. God calls these things abominations {Deuteronomy 18:10-12}, and He warns us to avoid them.

You who have read through the pages of *As Straight As An Arrow* now have no excuse but to try to resist the devil, for you are no longer ignorant of the fact that he uses deceit as his most important vantage point. But to strengthen your resolve to go and sin no more, you must put on the *full* armour of God, and that is done only by getting acquainted with God's Holy Word as found in the Bible. This is important because wisdom and honor come to those who dwell on God with all of their strength, mind, heart, and soul, but *dishonor* and *disgrace* come to those who dwell on the things of Satan.

Donning The Armour

Donning the full armour of God begins with humility of heart. Humility of heart is a more precious commodity than refiner's gold, for it is the opposite of pride and arrogance, which become heavy burdens to carry into the hereafter. So it is in reverence to God Almighty that we begin to don the armour...

As we place the *helmet* on our heads, we become aware that it provides us with the hope of salvation through just, honest, pure, and right thinking. Then as we place the *breastplate* (of righteousness) over our chests, we immediately see that it covers our most vital organ, the heart, and provides us with both faith and love to overcome fear and hatred. We then proceed to tighten the *belt* around our waists, and we come to understand that it holds the rest in place and enables us to "gird up our loins" in truth and justice. We then reach down and begin to place the *shoes* on, and we begin to realize that they will provide the protection that is necessary for our feet, which are eager to run the good race that is set before us. As we lace the final few laces, we begin to understand that we are not sprinters in this race of life, but rather marathon runners. And so we run the race patiently, proclaiming the good news of the gospel of Jesus Christ *every step of the way*. Then as we lift up the *shield* (of faith) our encouragement grows because the shield provides us with the protection we need to repel all the burning arrows that are shot at us by the Evil One. And then finally, as we take up the *sword* (which is the Word of God), we are now ready to go on the offensive; to strike back against the evil that surrounds us which has been propagated by Satan, the devil. This is the opposite of sitting idly by and watching the world that we live in go to hell in a hand basket!

Putting on the full Armour of God is vital to overcoming temptations, for as you have seen, we do not wrestle against flesh and blood, but against principalities, powers, the rulers of the darkness of this world, and against spiritual wickedness in high places.

Master Or Slave: *Your* Choice

Before the angel Lucifer became Satan the devil, he was full of wisdom and perfect in beauty, but he became proud and envious of God, instead of thankful to him. And thus Lucifer became a slave to his own desires, and has been so ever since. But let us not forget that this "King of the Slaves of Desire" is also the "Master of Deception" and he may be in our presence quite often.

No matter who we are or where we're at, Satan may be luring us into temptation. As we have seen, from the White House to the Churches, Satan knows no boundaries for the temptation of man. He even tempted the very Son of God, so what would make anyone think that *they* are above his approach? Unlike the rest of us, when Jesus was tempted, he remained steadfast and true, and refused to succumb to the temptations. This should make us realize (as I said before) that it is not a sin to be tempted, but it is indeed a sin to *flirt with* temptation.

Unlike Christ, we are weak, and much of the time we not only succumb to temptations, but we go hog-wild in our sins. Most of those who are now engulfed by sexual sin did not realize that in the beginning, when they first started flirting with certain temptations, that they would end up where they are this day— slaves to their greedy lusts for the flesh.

The sin of sexual immorality can lead to all manner of debauchery and can be compared to the actions of an ordinary leech. The leech is an aquatic or terrestrial worm that clings to the flesh of other creatures and sucks their blood until it becomes so full that it drops off. At times, the bloodsucking worm so engulfs itself in its lust for blood that it actually explodes! Like these creatures, sexual sin causes many people to be seeking ever more. They seek more and more and more... filling themselves up on the lust of the flesh...
never quite satisfied...
until...
(I think you get the picture).

Satan probably enjoys and is amused by people who lack self-control to such extremes as this, for he is diametrically opposed to the will of God. Our Creator is willful that *none* should perish, but that all should come to repentance. {2 Peter 3:9}. Satan, on the other hand, wants every single soul to turn away from God and serve their appetites instead. By succumbing to sins, they then become servants of Satan.

This is not what God had originally intended for his creation. He points out that even if one person in a hundred goes astray, that Jesus will go looking for that person with the hopes of bringing that *one* back to God, and he rejoices when he finds them!

The person who has gone astray and has engaged in the gay

lifestyle does not have to be forever a slave to the sin of sexual impurity. By putting their trust in God instead of in the weak flesh, they can find freedom and the peace of mind that comes with that freedom. Remember this: God makes a way of escape for *every* sin. It then becomes a choice as to whether that person remains steadfast in sin or escapes to freedom by putting on the full Armour of God.

**Put on the whole armour
of God, that you may be able
to stand against the wiles of the
devil.**

{Ephesians 6:11}

Chapter Seven

OVERCOMING THE WORLD

Through Faith

"...for the support of this Declaration, with a firm reliance on the protection of Divine Providence, we mutually pledge to each other our Lives, our Fortunes, and our sacred Honor."

Continental Congress 1776

OUR NATION IS EXPERIENCING WARFARE FROM within, and *you* have to choose which side you are on. The flesh wars against the Spirit, and the Spirit against the flesh; they are contrary to one another. So if you continue to do those immoral things that your body desires to do, you have chosen which side you are on. Likewise, if you resist those things that defile your body and mind, you too have chosen which side you are on. If you choose the latter, then you will also want to consider accepting Jesus Christ as your personal Lord and Savior, for *this* is the only way to stay the course.

America Is Engaged In Spiritual Warfare

When you accept Jesus into your heart and mind, you become a soldier that must be prepared for battle! When we talk about being prepared for battle for Christ, we are talking about *spiritual* warfare. In order to know what our goal in this war is, we must first understand where it is that we have been, where we are at now, and where we want to go from here. Instead of starting with where we once were, let me first mention that which is always on the front burner of everybody's mind practically all the time, and that is here and now; the *present*.

Without much doubt, we are living in what the Bible calls "the last days." When companies like the Disney Company produce pro-gay publications for teen-agers, advertise in pro-gay magazines such as the publication *Out*, produce anti-family and anti-Christian books and Satanic-themed music, and even go as far as to extend health care benefits to the live-in partners of their gay employees, while denying those same benefits to the non-married live-in partners of their straight employees...then we know we're in trouble!

The Bible gave us many obvious "clues" as to what the last days would be like. In describing those days it says that evil men and seducers shall wax worse and worse, deceiving and being deceived. There will be scoffers of the word of God. There will be those who promise liberty while they themselves are servants of corruption (whose minds have been blinded to the Gospel by Satan). There will be vain men who deceive many through their philosophies after the tradition of men and the rudiments of the world, and not after Christ. There will be false prophets. There will be preachers who in *word* publicly declare that they know God, but in *deed* they disown him. There will be wars and rumors of wars, famines, pestilence, earthquakes, increasing of lawlessness, and persecution of Christians. Men's hearts will fail them out of fear. People will be destroying the earth through pollution and waste. And the gospel of the Kingdom of God shall be preached in all the world for a witness to all nations...and then the end will come." {See Matthew 24:6-14, Luke 21:26, 2Corinthians 4:3-4, Colossians 2:8, 2Timothy 3:1-4, 13, Titus 1:16, 2Peter 2:19, and Revelation 11:18}.

The foregoing paragraph should be a wake-up call to all of us! Why? Because those who are in Christ will be rescued from the impending doom that is coming upon the earth. Those who are not, will not be. For this reason, those who know of the gospel should proclaim it. Those who are contemplating sin should think twice. And those who are self-confident in their sin should reconsider their position and repent, for they are in the most trouble!

The world sought to kill Jesus because of his claims. Today, nearly two thousand years later, the world still hates the *true* Christian. But even so, more and more people are coming to Christ, realizing that the throne of his mercy is their only hope of true salvation. When Christ overcame the principalities of darkness by making a show of them openly on the Cross, he revealed the key that unlocks the door to heaven's gates! He was manifested to destroy the works of the devil, and many people today *know* it.

One Nation Under God?

Every single one of us living here today is engaged in a war, and America is the battlefield. Indeed, besides murder, rape, and child molestation, the two most grotesque sins that have infiltrated our nation are the legalization of abortion and the gay rights movement. The latter two have occurred within just the past thirty years, and they have been allowed to permeate our once great nation due to propaganda and censorship.

If we want to turn this nation back into what it was just a while ago (one nation under God), then we should view the censoring of the Gospel as an act of war! Indeed, it has become spiritual warfare when nearly every one of the sitcoms on prime time television portray either antagonism, fornication, or homosexuality as all fine and dandy. Outside of Sunday morning sermons preached on TV, the major networks that air those prime time programs have *refused* to air messages from conservative Christian groups. They have deemed the material to be "too controversial" (which means in opposition to their own values and agendas). This should come as no surprise to those who know their Bible, for as mentioned earlier, it is written therein that Satan is the "Prince of the power of the air."

Now if we will take a brief moment to look at where we've been, we see that just a few years ago, it was just the opposite in this country. Sexual immorality was deemed inappropriate and it was highly frowned upon. Remember the *Dick Van Dyke* and *Lucy* shows, where even husbands and wives slept in separate beds? And *That Girl* Ann Marie (Played by actress Marlo Thomas), although a single woman in her 20's and making it on her own in New York, she couldn't dare give the impression that her and her boyfriend, Donald, were having any type of sexual contact. Yes, even ABC forbid that type of display at the time. Realizing that TV sends a message to kids on a weekly, if not daily basis, the creators and promoters of shows at that time upheld the integrity of good moral values.

Compare that to what we are seeing today. Regardless of the fact that a recent U.S. News and World Report poll showed that over eighty percent of our adult society is concerned about TV's references to sex outside marriage, and seventy-five percent of the people are concerned about the presentations of homosexuality, the promoters of these programs keep on spewing forth sexual immorality.

Yes, eight out of every ten adults believe that sex and sexual references on TV affect viewer behavior and contribute to the moral decline of this nation. But in spite of the overwhelming majority of the viewing audience's wishes to see programs clean up their act, the promoters are not only increasing the trash they put out, but they are also censoring anything that has to do with Christianity. For example, a Coral Ridge Ministries video documenting the pro-gay agenda, and yet how many have found freedom from the gay lifestyle (through faith in Christ) was blocked by the major TV networks across the country who refused to air the program! Around two hundred gay protesters marched in front of Coral Ridge Presbyterian Church in Fort Lauderdale, Florida in response to the video which, they said, promoted bigotry, lies, and hate. In fact, however, the program merely unveiled the hidden agenda of gay activists, and invited the lost to come to Christ for salvation and freedom from sexual slavery.

Now I don't want to totally bash the media or the TV stations, for there are some that have made great strides in a far better direction in the past few years. The two TV programs *Touched*

By An Angel and *Promised Land* are two examples. But still, for the most part, the opinions, immoral values, and false belief systems being expressed in the mass media today are *debunk.* They are null and void of all good reason. Why else would the National Association of Television Program Executives (NATPE) choose as the keynote speaker for their annual convention, so-called shock jock, Howard Stern? This is the man who, in wake of the tragic shooting deaths of fifteen high school students in Littleton, Colorado said "At least if you're going to kill yourself and kill all the kids, why wouldn't you have some sex?" (He was wandering why the killers didn't try to have sex with some of their high school student victims before they killed them.)

Regardless of this type of grievous behavior by TV executives, the followers of Christ are beginning to expose the lies for what they truly are. Even a cartoonist, in his own humorous way has gotten the message out from time-to-time in his *B.C.* column of the newspaper. In one recent column, the caveman character writes a message stating "Over here, one of our finest rights is freedom of the press." Then he sends it out over across the water in the hopes of receiving a reply. The next day, the message comes back from across the water with these words:

"Here too! Free to Censor...Free to Suppress...Free to Lie..."

Sound familiar? That's how the communist countries of the world have behaved. And now, it is happening right here in the good old US of A. Like those countries, what the biased mass media of this country is representing results only in the harm of those who follow after it. We can see examples of this in the recent wave of shooting incidents in our nation's schools. This is the type of result that a society gets when it alleviates itself from the Commandments of God and chooses instead to embrace an atheistic worldview. If we take a look back over the past century and a half, we can see this in the lives and words of people who have expressed this type of worldview.

A World Without God: A Message Of Despair
Ludwig Feuerbach, that German philosopher known for his

"contribution" to *materialism*, believed that religion was merely an unconscious product of the human imagination for myth making! He said "God and absolute reason are merely projections of the human mind." He believed that *Man*, in creating god in *his* own image, had "alienated himself from himself" by reducing himself to a small, evil creature who then needed to rely upon both Church and Government to guide him. Feuerbach said that if religion were abolished, people would overcome their "alienation." His writings, along with those of G.W.F. Hegel, greatly influenced the worldview of that German philosopher and revolutionist who produced the theories of modern Socialism and Communism, Karl Marx.

Marx, in his writing of *On the Jewish Question*, said Judaism and Christianity were "merely stages in the development of the human mind." He believed that "the imaginary world of religion" needed to be eliminated if mankind was to attain "political emancipation." Also famous for writing *Das Kapital*, Marx suffered from physical ailments for the last thirty-four years of his life, lived in poverty, and had marital problems.

Nobody knows for sure how many people perished during the purges of Soviet leader Joseph Stalin, who *absorbed the works of Marx*, but one thing for sure was that Stalin was puffed up by pride. He proclaimed himself as "a genius in all fields of human endeavor." And what did this "genius" provide for humanity? He ordered the operation of prison camps, execution grounds, and the brutal murder of what most historians have estimated to be between fourteen to twenty million of his own countrymen!

The world also had Arthur Schopenhauer, another German philosopher who believed that the will of man has no purpose; that it is pointless and negative. This "great wise man" wrote that expressions of the will are seen throughout nature in the struggles of animals, seeds, and magnets. He said that the only purpose of life is that of escaping the will and its painful strivings. Schopenhauer lived a life of solitude, resentful of the world's inability to recognize his "genius." His viewpoints did have consequences however. After his death in 1860, other atheists such as Freud and Nietzsche embraced his writings.

It was that Austrian neurologist who became the founder of

psychoanalysis, Sigmund Freud, who called religion a "universal neurosis" that had to be overcome if man was to attain "independence of mind." He tried to explain away God, prayer, (and religion in general) as neurotic feelings of dependence that stemmed from infancy. For the last sixteen years of his life until his death in 1939, Freud suffered from mouth cancer. Kind of ironic, don't you think?

Then we have that philosophical writer, Friedrich Nietzsche, who in his infamous book *Thus Spoke Zarathustra,* wrote that "God is dead." In that book, Nietzche's main character "Zarathustra" says that man made his way from worm to man, and that man was ever evolving into the "overman"—a super being far superior to modern man. He said that as "ape is a painful embarrassment to modern man, so will it be that modern man will be an embarrassment to the overman."

If one takes a brief look at this book that Nietzsche wrote, they will see that it celebrates Socrates' way of dying (he was forced to take poison) as opposed to the way Jesus died on the cross, teaches earth worship, talks about an "ass festival" and completely and utterly mocks God. Perhaps that is the reason the book became so popular in some small circles of society. (We will always have our Sodom and Gomorrah residents, at least until Christ returns to set up his New World Order that is.)

That you may know the ending to the story; Mr. Nietzsche did not live to see his book's success. He became insane from the disease of syphilis as a result of his gay lifestyle, and was admitted to an asylum where he spent the last eleven years of his life unaware of the book's main publication. His family even halted the first publication of the book for fear of being charged with blasphemy (a criminal offense at the time).

God is not mocked without great repercussions being felt! Thus that homosexual atheist who wrote that God is dead, became an insane and broken man, and died in 1900 and was buried in the ground where he became food for worms... meanwhile *God lives on.*

Which brings us to Adolf Hitler, who absorbed both Darwin's "survival of the fittest" theory and Nietzsche's "overman" rubbish. The Holocaust (which is an Old Testament sacrificial term used by historians) that resulted in the massacre of some six million Jews by Hitler's Nazi regime between 1933 and 1941, was the result of Hitler's worldview of what he believed to be "a need for a super race."

Years later, now that the tragic results are in and the numbers have been tallied, we find that the worldview of men such as these resulted in the hideous torture and deaths of somewhere around *twenty-five million* innocent men, women, and children. How sad indeed.

But we're not finished yet. The atheistic worldview has had other consequences too. Bertrand Russell, who was another atheist philosopher, wrote *Why I Am Not a Christian* in 1957, and said that those who tried to prove the existence of God had "failed" because their arguments were not based on logic. The argument for design, as he put it, "was destroyed by Darwin." Another mocker of God, Russell said "I do not think Christ was the wisest of men..." and "...in matters of wisdom and virtue, I put Buddha and Socrates above him (Christ)..." Russell was one of those who helped usher in the progressive schools (where religion is avoided). Like Darwin, he also helped to usher in conflict between science and religion based upon his misinterpretation of *true* science. But Russell, who failed in his home life (he was married four times) said later in his life that the opinions he had expressed earlier on were ideas that seemed sensible at the time, but that he would be surprised if "...subsequent research did not show that modification would be necessary." He spent his last years writing about gloom and doom, and the despair he felt about the future of mankind. He died in 1970.

Madalyn Murray O'Hair (another atheist who believed that the word of God should not be taught to our children in school) fought to have Bible reading and the Lord's Prayer banned from our public schools through the courts, and she succeeded. She then went on and published the magazine *American Atheist* and formed the group known as "American Atheists." But her own son, Bill, saw a better side to life. He broke with his mother's godless worldview, and wrote a book about his early life with her. He entitled it *My Life Without God.*

We can see from the above examples that the atheistic worldview (and its subsequent actions) leads to one conclusion— *despair.* In contrast, those who believe upon God and meditate upon *his* word have better things to say.

The Christian Message: A Message Of Hope

When the atheists of America pour out their godless message across our land, the followers of Christ counter with the *truth.* As Jesus Christ himself said: "A good tree brings forth not corrupt fruit; neither does a corrupt tree bring forth good fruit. For every tree is known by his own fruit. For of thorns men do not gather figs, nor of a bramble bush gather they grapes. A good man out of the good treasure of his heart brings forth that which is good: and an evil man out of the evil treasure of his heart brings forth that which is evil: for out of the abundance of the heart his mouth speaks." {Luke 6:43-45}.

Noah Webster, known as the "Schoolmaster of the Nation" was a statesman, educator, lexicographer and the author of *Webster's Dictionary.* He wrote: "The Bible is the Chief moral cause of all that is good, and the best corrector of all that is evil in human society...It is extremely important to our nation, in a political as well as religious view, that all possible authority and influence should be given to the scriptures, for these furnish the best principles of *civil liberty,* and the most effectual support of republican government...The man, therefore, who weakens or destroys the divine authority of *that* Book may be accessory to all the public disorders which society is doomed to suffer..." (Emphasis added). The so-called American *Civil Liberties* Union stands both in mockery of this great man's words of religious content, and in proof of the soundness of those very words!

Another famous Webster, Daniel, the American politician and diplomat whose political career spanned nearly forty years (during which he served as a U.S. Congressman, a U.S. Senator, and as the Secretary of State for three different Presidents), and who is considered one of the greatest orators in American history said this: "If we abide by the principles taught in the Bible, our country will go on prospering and to prosper; but if we and our posterity neglect its instructions and authority, no man can tell how sudden a catastrophe may overwhelm us and bury all our glory in profound obscurity."

Henry Ward Beecher, the famous American editor, abolitionist, and clergyman who increasingly used his pulpit to denounce civil corruption wrote these things: "A Christian is nothing but a sinful man who has put himself to school to Christ for the honest purpose of becoming better. Christianity works while infidelity talks. She feeds the hungry, clothes the naked, visits and cheers the sick, and seeks the lost, while infidelity abuses her and babbles nonsense and profanity. 'I can forgive but I cannot forget' is only another way of saying 'I cannot forgive.' The Bible is God's chart for you to steer by...."

Christopher Columbus, who was ridiculed, rejected, and laughed at for his desire to sail to the new world (the Indies), wrote in his *Libro de las profecias* (Book of prophecies) "...there is no question that the inspiration was from the Holy Spirit...The fact that the gospel must still be preached to so many lands in such a short time, *that* is what convinces me."

Ralph Waldo Emerson, the famous American poet and essayist who wrote the *Concord Hymn* in 1836, a poem which made famous the Revolutionary War battle at Concord, Massachusetts with the phrase "the shot heard around the world" acknowledged this: "All I have seen has taught me to trust the Creator for all I have not seen."

Machael Faraday, the English chemist and naturalist and one of the greatest physicists of all time (he discovered electrolysis, electromagnetic induction, etc., and invented the first electrical generator in 1831), whose writings profoundly inspired Thomas Edison, wrote this: "The Christian religion is a revelation, and that revelation is the Word of God."

George H. Gallup, the famous American pollster said "I could prove God statistically. Take the human body alone—the chances that all the functions of an individual would just happen is a statistical monstrosity."

Victor Hugo, that famous French author who wrote *The Hunchback of Notre Dame* in 1831, and numerous other great works such as *Les Miserables* and *Legend of the Centuries* was deeply involved in politics. He avowed: "England has two books, the Bible and Shakespeare. England made Shakespeare, but the Bible made England."

Hans Christian Anderson, a Danish novelist who wrote among others *The Ugly Duckling, The Emperor's New Clothes,* and *The Tinder Box* wrote in his autobiography: "The different periods of my life passed before me. I knelt down upon the stage and repeated our Lord's Prayer...Humility and prayer unto God for strength to deserve happiness, filled my heart. May He always enable me to preserve these feelings."

Are these—from the statesmen and scientists to the writers, and poets and many other professions and callings in-between— the intolerant, judgmental hate mongers that some would have us to believe?

Personally, I do not believe that in the truest sense of the word, that there really are any atheists. I base this belief on circumstantial evidence. The evidence being that if the self-professed "atheist" is placed upon a sinking boat in shark infested waters—and there is no help in sight—I believe that he or she will pray to God for help. I could be wrong, but I'm not the only one who believes this way. I think atheism was summed up best by General Douglas MacArthur when he simply said "There are no atheists in the foxholes of Bataan."

Indeed, there are times when the so-called atheists' disbelief in God will abandon them. Nevertheless, until *that* time comes into their lives, there will still be those who will continue to enthusiastically voice their non-belief in the hope that they can influence others to feel the same way. As you have seen however, there are those who do believe upon God and rest their hopes in his son, and I believe that they have a better tale to tell, a better song to sing, and they too cannot and *will not* remain silent.

The First Act Of Congress

Yes overcoming the world is done by faith, but it is also done by expounding the truth which often (if not always) involves *exposing* the lies. The Scriptures tell us to always be ready to give an answer to every man that asks, of the hope that is in us. With this in mind, we must first come to a better understanding of our history (and the truth *of it*) that is day-by-day being purged by the Master of Deception. He has given an agenda to his followers, and it involves brainwashing our forthcoming generations into believing that a secular humanistic worldview is best. Following his lead, they are attempting to expurgate all mention of God and Christ from our history books, from our speeches, and from our ceremonies—in short, from our *culture.* Outside of TV programming, it doesn't take much to realize how far we (as a nation) have fallen in a short period of time. For example, how many people today, especially school students realize that the very first act of our Continental Congress was to pray? When the members of Congress met on September 6, 1774 to chart the course of the new country they were giving birth to, one of the members made a motion that the meeting should be opened with prayer. Although first opposed by two other members due to the division of religious sects among members (although nearly all were Christian based), Sam Adams stood and declared "I'm no bigot, and I can hear a prayer from any gentleman of piety and virtue who is a friend to his country." And Adam's motion was seconded and then passed in the affirmative. The prayer went like this:

"Be Thou present, O' God of Wisdom, and direct the counsel of the honorable assembly. Enable them to settle all things on the best and surest foundations, that the scenes of blood may be speedily closed, that order, harmony, and peace may be effectually restored, and truth and justice, religion and piety prevail and flourish among the people. Preserve the health of their bodies, and the vigor of their minds; shower down on the millions they represent here, such temporal blessings as Thou seest expedient for them in this world, and crown them with everlasting glory in the world to come. All this we ask in the name and through the merits of Jesus Christ, Thy Son, and our Savior, Amen!"

And thus the first official act of Congress, *prayer* became the first act of *each session* of Congress. And later, the framers of the Constitution (of which 36 of 55 had been members of the Continental Congress) relied upon God as well, as is shown by their writings and documents.

Today, groups like the ACLU have changed the Constitution into a radically different document—one that separates religion from politics.

The Lie Of "Separation Of Church And State"

The First Amendment to the Constitution which states "Congress shall make no law respecting an establishment of religion, or prohibiting the free exercise thereof." was meant, by its writers, that Congress shall not dictate or ordain any one *Christian* sect (denomination) over any other *Christian* sect. The designers of the Constitution had different denominations, but all were basically Christian. During the time that this document was written, polls indicated that *ninety-eight percent of this nation* believed itself to be Christian!

The secular humanists that have crept into this nation since that time have jumped all over the First Amendment and have twisted its meaning to suit their own purposes! As Herbert W. Titus stated "They (groups like the ACLU) have basically said that religion has no place in the public arena of our nation, even though historically it was the very foundation and framework of our life, our liberty, and our law."

That the majority of American students do not know the rich Christian foundation that their ancestors laid for this nation, nor the principles that they strove to live by, shows just how bad our public education system has become. So once again, let's separate truth from error.

When President Thomas Jefferson wrote in a letter in 1802 to the Danbury Baptist Association of Danbury, Connecticut referencing a wall of separation between Church and State, he was assuring them that the "wall" was a one-way wall of protection *for* the church *from* government interference, *not the other way around!* He was basically reaffirming that the federal government would not single out any single Christian denomination over the others as a *national* denomination. The letter he wrote to those Baptists meant precisely that, and it was no part of the First Amendment to the Constitution whatsoever! In fact, the First Amendment was written thirteen years earlier.

Jefferson's reverence for God is found in abundance in his writings, but the secular humanistic viewpoints of just a handful of people in positions of power have perverted the minds of the masses with their lies. They would have us to believe that Jefferson was not a religious man, and that the Constitution is void of Christian integrity. This is nothing short of a farce—a sham—and apathetic America has bought into it! The "high and impregnable wall between church and state" was actually written by Supreme Court Justice Hugo Black (who had once been a member of the Ku Klux Klan) at the prodding of an ACLU lawyer named Leo Pfeffer. In 1947 Pfeffer wrote the draft for *Everson v. Board of Education*. In that draft, Pfeffer referred to Jefferson's letter, and then added his own twist to it. And, with Justice Black's interpretation and a 5-4 vote, the Supreme Court concocted the lie. Thus one ACLU lawyer, one atheist judge, and one vote that went the wrong way now dictated that America would henceforth keep God out of government sponsored affairs, including the educational system.

It should be obvious to any *thinking* person that the wall of separation between Church and State that is being used today to remove the vestiges of Christian religious expression is, in short, a crock of bull! It is a lie of the highest order that has been concocted by Satan to con the American people into believing that religious expression should not be tolerated in public places; that it is a "threat" to democracy. Those who are promoting the gay lifestyle have recognized this, and they are now trying to capitalize on it.

But once again, let's set the record straight. By studying the *historical records* of our nation, we see that without exception, the Constitutions of all fifty states contain an appeal (or a prayer) to Almighty God. Imagine that.

A History Lesson From Our Presidents

Nearly every President that this nation has ever had has realized the importance of Christianity in America. If we listen to many of them, we hear words such as "Of all the dispositions and habits which lead to political prosperity, Religion and Morality are indispensable supports." Thus spoke George Washington, our *very first* President. Washington also said "Reason and experience both forbid us to expect that national morality can prevail in exclusion of religious principle." Imagine that.

Our second President, John Adams had this to say: "We have no government armed with power capable of contending with human passions unbridled by morality and religion." He also said this: "Our Constitution was made only for a moral and religious people. It is wholly inadequate for the government of any other." Imagine that.

Contrary to what our atheist friends would have us believe, our third President, Thomas Jefferson, not only penned the words of the Declaration of Independence which appeals to God, the Creator, Divine Providence, and the Supreme Judge of the world, but he also personally introduced a resolution calling for a Day of Fasting and Prayer while he was the Governor of Virginia. Jefferson also wrote many letters to his friends that reflected upon his faith in God. In his Notes on the State of Virginia he said: "God who gave us life gave us liberty. And can the liberties of a nation be thought secure when we have removed their only firm basis, a conviction in the minds of the people that these liberties are of the Gift of God? That they are not to be violated but with His wrath? Indeed, I tremble for my country when I reflect that God is just; that His justice cannot sleep forever." Imagine that.

Abraham Lincoln, our sixteenth president, said, wrote, and delivered so many speeches about God and the Bible that it would be impossible for us to count them all. If *this* man, whose speeches and writings were deemed *the best* among American presidents by literary critics and historians alike, were to run for office today, he would be considered by liberal activists as a far right-wing extremist and a religious zealot. The gay community would probably even consider him a *bigot!* Thus the white man who fought for and won the freedom of black slaves would be considered an intolerant man because his views would not coincide with those of the gay activists of America.

As President, Lincoln issued a National Day of Prayer and Fasting, a National Day of Thanksgiving, and his last act of Congress required that the motto "In God We Trust" be inscribed upon all our national currency. Imagine that.

Moving right along, listen to the words of our eighteenth President, Ulysses S. Grant, as he quoted from the book of Proverbs: "Righteousness exalts a nation; but sin is a reproach to any people."

Our twentieth president, James Garfield said "...the people are responsible for the character of their Congress. If that body be ignorant, reckless and corrupt, it is because the people tolerate ignorance, recklessness and corruption. If it be intelligent, brave and pure, it is because the people demand these high qualities to represent them in the national legislature..."

Our twenty-sixth President, Theodore Roosevelt warned us when he said: "Every thinking man realizes the teachings of the Bible are so interwoven and entwined with our whole civic and social life that it would be literally impossible for us to figure ourselves what that life would be if these standards were removed. We would lose almost all the standards by which we now judge both public and private morals; all the standards towards which we strive to raise ourselves."

Roosevelt also said "Progress has brought us both unbounded opportunities and unbridled difficulties. Thus, the measure of our civilization will not be that we have done much, but what we have done with that much. I believe that the next half-century will determine if we will advance the cause of Christian civilization or revert to the horrors of brutal paganism. The thought of modern industry in the hands of Christian charity is a dream worth dreaming. The thought of industry in the hands of paganism is a nightmare beyond imagining. The choice between the two is upon us."

He also once stated: "...in occupying an exalted position in the nation, I am enabled to preach the practical moralities of the Bible to my fellow-countrymen and to hold up Christ as the hope and Savior of the world."

In their fight to keep religion out of the public arena, how would groups like the ACLU be able to explain these statements if Roosevelt were president today?

Woodrow Wilson, our twenty-eighth President said this: "A nation which does not remember what it was yesterday, does not know what it is today, nor what it is trying to do. We are trying to do a futile thing if we do not know where we came from or what we have been about...The Bible...is the one supreme source of revelation of the meaning of life, the nature of God and spiritual nature and needs of men. It is the only guide of life which really leads the spirit in the way of peace and salvation. America was born a Christian nation. America was born to exemplify that devotion to the elements of righteousness which are derived from the revelations of Holy Scripture."

The other Roosevelt, our thirty-second President, Franklin D., said this: "We cannot read the history of our rise and development as a nation, without reckoning with the place the Bible has occupied in shaping the advances of the Republic... Where we have been the truest and most consistent in obeying its precepts, we have attained the greatest measure of contentment and prosperity."

Our thirty-fifth President, John Fitzgerald Kennedy said "The rights of man come not from the generosity of the state but from the hand of God."

Our thirty-eighth President, Gerald Ford said: "Without God there could be no American form of government, nor an American way of life."

Our thirty-ninth President, James Earl Carter said "We believe that the first time we're born as children, it is human life given to us; and when we accept Jesus as our Savior, it's a new life. That's what *born again* means."

And our forty-first President, George Bush had this to say: "The great faith that led our Nation's Founding Fathers to pursue this bold experience in self-government has sustained us in uncertain and perilous times; it has given us strength and inspiration to this very day. Like them, we do very well to recall our 'firm reliance on the protection of Divine Providence' to give thanks for the freedom and prosperity this Nation enjoys, and to pray for continued help and guidance from our wise and loving Creator."

From our Founding Fathers to our Presidents, from George Washington to George Bush, these men have lived their lives with an inner peace that can only be had by a hope, a belief, and a faith in a better world to come—a world that will be governed, not by a president, but by a king. That king is the King of Kings, the Prince of Peace, and the one who overcame the world on the cross of Calvary.

Sitting On The Fence

The evidence is clear to all those who know the truth and are willing to step back and take a real hard look at what is happening all around us in view of The Big Picture. That evidence points to the fact that the Bible's prophetic messages are coming to pass *right before our very eyes!*

The Bible tells us that it is by the hand of God that men receive their power and position of authority over nations. The form of government instituted in this nation was meant (by its designers) to be one that adhered to God's Laws and propagated the Christian way of life. Since this country has prospered as none other, it is obviously a sign of God's approval! Up until recently, men who believed in this original meaning for the people were put in authority over our nation. But now we are being led by men of evil intent, and America is beginning to reap the rewards of profligacy due to the apathy of her citizens. Focus On The Family's Shirley Dobson has commented that the "Secular humanists have the White House, they have the Legislative, Executive, and Judicial branches... they have the entertainment industry, the media, and the public schools. They have the ears of every institution (that governs our lives) *except* the Church and the Family." And she's right! By targeting the sacred institution of marriage, the gay rights activists are now trying to infiltrate the traditional family unit structure as well. And all of this has happened over the past few years because too many members of the Church have separated themselves from the political process that once made this country great. The gay rights agenda has moved forward, while Christians have sat on their hands and watched the country become something that would have our forefathers turning in their graves! As the Claremont Institute recently stated "Most of the demands of the 1972 Gay Rights Platform have now been met."

America has become a lazy nation! We don't tend to act until things reach the crisis stages. Today most of our church-going members seem to prefer a "fast-food God" who can be paid a penny's worth of devotion in return for a pound's worth of diplomatic dignity from their fellowman! But God is not to be trifled with! In His word, he has stated that faith without works is *dead*. {James 2:20}. He has also stated that of those whose works are neither cold nor hot, but are lukewarm, he will spew them out of his mouth! {Revelation 3:15-16}. So those who compromise with the world when it comes to the unchanging word of God are going to find out that the one true God of the Universe brings all people to a fork in the road, and says "Choose!"   And the signposts read...

Obedience (Christ)
O T H E R (Satan)

One path is narrow, and few tend to choose it. The other path is wide, and many go its way. There are no other roads. There is no in-between ground to stand on. And so it is with you. You must choose which direction *you* will follow.

Presidential candidate, Alan Keyes has put it this way: "I believe that it is more than time that we make Americans realize that we do, in this generation face a choice. We are either going to let the Declaration [Of Independence] and its principles fade into oblivion and, with it, I believe, the hope of American freedom, or we are going to reclaim those principles by boldly asserting that we have the right to believe and to assert and to speak about the religious basis and foundation that the Declaration represents."

Gay activists are boldly asserting themselves. The bias liberal media is aggressively asserting their viewpoints. The ACLU, activist judges, and others in high places are doing the same. But are *Christians?*

I believe that if the followers of Christ do not get active behind their faith and come forward to publicly rebuke this sin of homosexuality, that our nation is going to be severely punished by God. This is almost as certain as night follows day.

Why? Because throughout history when the people defiled themselves upon the lands which the Lord had given them to dwell in, God visited their iniquities, and the lands themselves vomited out the inhabitants thereof! As someone else once said, "If God doesn't punish America, he's going to have to apologize to the residents of Sodom and Gomorrah!"

You have now seen how our country was founded by, and should be a Christian nation. Throughout this book you will have learned how The Mayflower Compact, The Declaration of Independence, The Northwest Ordinance, and The Constitution all support this conclusion. You will have had the blinders of deceit removed, and will have been awakened to the truth of the subtle (yet progressive) gay rights movement occurring in America today. That movement is both antagonistic and hostile towards Christianity. We are seeing proofs of that nearly every day. As D. James Kennedy, one of the leading Christian statesmen of our times has so aptly put it "Your vote—stolen. Your rights—taken away. Your Christian freedoms—crushed. Bit by bit...it is happening."

Knowing all this, will you not now *do* something about it?

It is time, my friend, for the people of God to speak out against this great sin that is taking place in America today, and in the process, reform this country. There are many ways to go about doing just that.* Remember this; our duly elected members of Congress, from the President on down, are just that...duly elected. They are supposed to represent our views, for they are *our* servants. If we don't like the job they've been performing, then it's up to us to "fire" them, and to hire somebody who will reflect our values and viewpoints. Nothing less will do.

*Some of the resources listed in the back of this book can help those readers who desire to see our nation restored to its Godly foundational principles. See pages 196 to 204.

Reclaiming Our Nation: Through Prayer

Yes, the time has come to push back the deception that has

led to this sinful lifestyle, which has been spreading out across our land like a billowy dark cloud. Throughout this book, mention has been made of many of the organizations that are backing the gay rights movement. But now let me once again remind you that back of all this *is* Satan and his demonic forces. He has deceived these groups, these *people*, into believing the lie that this is something that is unavoidable—that it is not a sin— that it is a genetic character trait, and that it should therefore be accepted and tolerated completely by society.

Knowing that we are not wrestling against flesh and blood, but instead against spiritual wickedness in high places, we should understand that one of the most effective weapons we can use in the war against this sin is prayer. Yes, you heard it right! The followers of Christ are told (in Scripture) to be humble, gentle, and patient. We are told to show our love by being tolerant with one another. We are told to do our best to preserve the unity which the Spirit gives by means of the peace that binds us together. And, we are told to *pray without ceasing*. Why are we told to pray without ceasing? Because, as the epistle of James tells us, "The effectual fervent prayer of a righteous man availeth much" {James 5:16}.

If our motives are right and our hearts in the right places, our prayers are placed on a beam of sunlight and they travel upwards...penetrating the clouds, the darkness, and the atmosphere. They travel ever upwards through the outer space until they penetrate even the heavens. And there, they reach the ears of Almighty God. And all this happens in a split second!

Because of our faith we pray to God, for we know that our Father in heaven hears our prayers, and knows our hearts. For example, in the Old Testament book of Second Chronicles we find that Solomon prayed fervently, and he backed his prayers with *action*. And the Lord appeared to Solomon by night, and said unto him, "I have heard thy prayer..."
And the Lord went on to say...

"If my people, which are called by my name, shall humble themselves, and pray, and seek my face, and turn from their wicked ways; then will I hear from heaven, and will forgive their sin, and will heal their land." {2Chronicles 7:14}.

I believe that this passage is referring not only to the people of Solomon's day, but to the body of Christ in general. It is one of the greatest examples of the effects of prayer given in the Bible.

Yes, *prayer* is the prescription for healing our land! It is the medicine that is given for healing the heart, and by no other means can we change our nation, in the long run, than by changing the heart of the nation—one person at a time.

Reclaiming Our Nation: One Heart At A Time

There is but one body and one Spirit just as there is one hope to which God has called us. There is one Lord, one faith, one baptism, and one God and Father of all mankind who is Lord of all...works through all...and is in all. Each one of us has received a special gift in proportion to what Christ has given. As the Scripture says, "When he ascended up on high he led captivity captive, and gave gifts unto men." {Ephesians 4:8}.

Now, what does "he ascended up on high" mean? It means that he first descended into the lower parts of the earth. He that descended is that same one who ascended up far above all the heavens that he might fill all things. It was he who gave gifts to mankind. He appointed some to be apostles, others to be prophets, others to be evangelists, others to be pastors and teachers. He did this to prepare all God's people for the work of Christian service in order to build up the body of Christ.

The Word of God tells us that we are to be renewed in the spirit of our minds. We are to speak that which is good to the use of edifying, so that it may minister grace to those who hear it. And we are not to grieve the Holy Spirit of God. We are not to utter the name of the Lord in vain, for there are those who profess the Holy Spirit but deny the power thereof. We are also to let go of all bitterness, wrath, anger, and clamor, and instead be kind and tenderhearted to one another, and forgive one another...as God has forgiven us...through Christ. We are to be forgiving and gentle with those who are living the gay lifestyle; which is to say *we are to be understanding.* We have to understand that they have been deceived. This is not the same as saying that we should be tolerant of homosexual sin. Tolerant of people—

yes. Tolerant of sin—no. We have not been called to bicker with them. We should, however, tell them the truth in a loving way. This is one of the very things that the Church has been instructed to do.

As Christians, shall we all come together to that unity of the faith, and in our knowledge of the Son of God? Shall we become mature people, reaching to the stature of the fullness of Christ? Shall we then no longer be lead into error through the deceitfulness of others, but instead, by speaking the truth in love, grow up in every way into Christ who is the head? And shall we (as we are commissioned to do) go out and proclaim the good news, the gospel of our Lord throughout the land? *Let us pray that we will!* Let us pray that God will give us both the courage and the ability to express grace (even when we are under pressure) to be up to the task. For these are the very things that will enable us to reclaim our nation...one heart at a time!

Reclaiming Our Nation: Through Truth Awareness

If you have been keeping up on current events involving the gay rights movement, then you have undoubtedly witnessed the uprising of Christian leaders and their call for the followers of Christ to stand tall together against this evil influence upon our society. Many in the Christian Community have been doing just that. They are speaking up for Truth, with a capital "T".

For example, in response to the backlash felt by those public figures (such as Reggie White) that were mentioned earlier, in July, 1998, an ad campaign designated to showing people who are living the gay lifestyle that they can change—through the healing power of Jesus Christ—was released to some of the nation's major newspapers. Eighteen pro-family organizations banded together to get the truth out. They entitled the articles the "Truth in Love" campaign. Major publications including *Newsweek, Time, U.S. News & World Report,* and the *Wall Street Journal* all featured articles in response to the ads. The newspaper ads also stirred up enough attention that some television broadcasts such as *Face the Nation, Good Morning America, Nightline, The McLaughlin Group,* and *The Today Show* hit the airwaves with responses.

One of the ads released by the campaign showed a picture of hundreds of people (who had *formerly* lived the gay lifestyle) all gathered together in Seattle to celebrate the freedom from sexual bondage that they had found through Jesus Christ. In all, over eight hundred people showed up with their message of hope.

Janet Folger, who battled against abortion as the former legislative director for Ohio Right to Life, is now the national director for the Center for Reclaiming America, one of the groups who formed the Truth in Love ad campaign. After a swift and hostile reaction to the ads from both the gay community and liberals alike, Folger stated "On the abortion issue, choice is worshipped by the left. On Truth in Love, we're offering choice and being slammed for it...Go figure."

Even though they have been charged with all manner of accusations, the supporters of the ads have remained undaunted, and the Truth in Love Ad Campaign has continued. In May, 1999, the campaign began to reach out into the TV market through commercial ad spots. The first commercial aired in the nation's capital and provided a mother, her son, and an urgent message. It showed Frances Johnston and her son, Michael. Michael Johnston formerly lived the gay lifestyle, and as a result contracted AIDS. In the compassionate commercial, Mrs. Johnston speaks plainly about her son's past behavior, and she advises other mothers "If you love your children, love them enough to let them know the truth... My son Michael found out the truth, but he found out too late."

Michael Johnston found out too late that he was living a lie. But he did find Jesus Christ. Now, he enthusiastically ministers to others who are living the type of lifestyle that he once lived. And because he came to accept Jesus Christ as his personal Lord and Savior, Michael now has an *eternal* reward...which means he will live much, much longer than those who have no such diseases—but who don't have Christ!

Fighting The Good Fight

Janet Parshall is a radio talk show host, and is the national spokesperson for the Washington-based Family Research Council. Janet unashamedly declares Jesus Christ. She also fights against evil works in high places. For instance, when Senator Edward Kennedy reintroduced ENDA, Janet Parshall came to the forefront and told the American people the truth about this bill. She said "Under this bill, employers who hold moral objections to homosexuality are required, by force of the federal government, to keep their convictions in the closet."

Janet Parshall has also spoken out against the judicial tyranny that has now taken place in America. She has said that "Past practice confirms the authority of Congress to challenge judges when their rulings threaten constitutional self-government." "The founders of our nation feared that if any one branch of government seized supreme authority to control the meaning of the Constitution, that branch would gradually expand its own powers and encroach on the legitimate authority of the other branches. This is why the founders crafted the Constitution around the idea of a balance and separation of powers, not on executive, legislative, or judicial supremacy."

Robert Knight is also one who is not afraid to speak out against the deception that has been going on. Knight was one of several witnesses who gave testimony during the Senate hearing regarding the proposal of the Hate Crimes Prevention Act (HCPA). "It sets up special classes of victims who are afforded a higher level of government protection than others victimized by similar crimes, violating the concept of equal protection; it politicizes criminal prosecutions... it would have a chilling effect on free speech by making unpopular ideas a basis for harsher treatment in criminal proceedings." Knight said. He went on to say that the aim of gay activists "...seems to be to silence all opposition to acceptance of homosexuality."

The American Family Association, another pro-family group opposed to the bill because of its sexual orientation provision, said that (HCPA) would "...bring the full power of federal law to bear against individuals and organizations that publicly address religious or pro-marriage views that homosexuality is wrong."

Despite the recent passage of the hate crimes bill in the Senate, the Christian message is indeed making a difference. In

April 1998, for example, the announcement came that the ABC Television Network would not be carrying the *Ellen* sitcom any more. ABC had been feeling the pressure from concerned citizens and pro-family groups that *Ellen* was not something that their children should be watching, and the program's ratings dropped. The May 8th edition of *Entertainment Weekly* carried a cover picture of Ellen DeGeneres and the words "Yep, She's Too Gay" on it. Apparently ABC felt that Ellen had went too far with her pro-gay agenda, and wasn't so funny anymore. So much for it "being cool to be gay in Hollywood" as the *National Enquirer* tabloid had proclaimed earlier.

Due to the active stance also taken by pro-family groups and others, Dr. Raymond Fowler, the American Psychological Association's Executive Director, retracted his organization's stance on the article that was published in their *Psychological Bulletin* about pedophilia not being harmful to children. The organization did an about face on the article and also adopted a resolution that condemns all sexual relations between adults and children.

Christian political activism has (as mentioned earlier) also stopped legalized same-sex marriages from taking place in this country...so far.

Indeed, fighting the good fight *can* make a difference. We can reclaim our nation...by praying...by expressing grace under pressure...and by enthusiastically getting the truth out. And by making a difference in this country, we will make a difference in the world at large, because most other nations tend to take their cue by looking to the actions of America first.

The "Wall" Comes Tumbling Down

If you take a look at the documents that formed the foundational guiding principles for America, you will find that the *Mayflower Compact* says that the main reason for the Pilgrims coming here was to advance the Kingdom and Gospel of Christ. They set out to build a "city on a hill" to provide a model for godly living for the rest of the world.

You will also find that within the *Constitution of the New England Confederation* these words are written: "We all came into these parts of America with the same end and aim, namely, to advance the Kingdom of our Lord Jesus Christ and to enjoy the liberties of the Gospel in purity with peace."

When you look at the law of the *Northwest Ordinance*, you will see that when it was passed, it stated "Religion, Morality, and Knowledge being necessary to good government and the happiness of mankind, schools and the means of education shall *forever* be encouraged." (Emphasis added).

If you leaf through the *Declaration of Independence*, the basic document of the birthright of our nation itself, right away you see how it mentions God in the very first paragraph.

And if you do a little legwork, and study the political science of America, you may be surprised to learn that even our current form of government was derived from the Bible itself! Our Founding Fathers got their idea for it from the writings of a French political philosopher named Charles Montesquieu, who laid out the plan for a government that would have its powers divided into three branches.

Judicial branch = The Lord is our Judge.
Legislative branch = The Lord is our Lawgiver.
Executive branch = The Lord is our King.

Montesquieu derived his idea from the Old Testament book of Isaiah 33:22. Imagine that! If you doubt this statement, check it out for yourself. Here we have the current governmental system under which we operate and live our lives, and its very conception came straight from the pages of the Holy Bible! Unfortunately, the system has not retained its integrity. It has now become corrupted by evil men who place money and sex before God, and because for too long now, there has been a serious lack of Christian involvement in the political process.

The trumpets of truth are, however, beginning to reemerge. If the American people will hear and give heed to the alarms that are once again being sounded, then the faith of the good and God-fearing citizens will produce the actions that are needed to reverse this corruption of governmental power. Indeed, if the truth of our Nation's rich Christian heritage and its historical role in our politics and government is not suppressed nor subverted, *then* the pillars of the "wall" of separation between Church and State (as it is misconstrued today) will crack, and like the walls of that ancient city Jerico, when the priests blew their trumpets and the Israelites shouted out loud...it will crumble...and fall! For it was by *faith* that the walls of Jerico fell down after the Israelites had marched around them for seven days. And it is by *faith* that this wall too will come tumbling down. Then we will once again become "one nation under God."

Running The Good Race

The first step to overcoming the world (and the evil therein) is to place one's faith in the only one who has overcome *all* temptations. Jesus Christ overcame every temptation that we have had or ever will have, and he overcame the world through his death on the cross.

The second step to overcoming the world is to overcome one's own temptations by putting on the full armour of God, which we have already discussed.

The third and final step to overcoming the world is to run with patience the race that is set before us. Running the good race is living a life in which we strive for *endurance* and against the *ego*, for the world is passing away, but they that do the will of God will abide forever!

When we take in knowledge of God, we gain a better understanding of what is true, honest, pure, peaceful, gentle, just, friendly, and full of compassion. The wisdom from above produces a harvest of good deeds, and it is free from prejudice and hypocrisy. Indeed, being not conformed to this world involves *transformation*—it involves the renewing of our minds through that wisdom from above.

And so we are to be sober, be vigilant, resist evil by remaining steadfast in the faith, and show mercy because our neighbors experience the same trials that we experience. We are to think upon things of good report. We are to think upon things of virtue. It is common sense to realize that thinking upon these things will produce good reactions. But how can one who fills their mind with pornographic materials expect to react in any way other than pornographic?

With this, we come to realize that true sufficiency comes only from God. In other words, if you will lean not unto your own understanding, but yield to the power of God instead, then he will clean you up. What it all boils down to is a test of one's faith, and an all-important question arises:

Is there really a God in heaven who has given us his word, and are there really rewards and unspeakable joys reserved for those who overcome the trials and tribulations of this life?

Abel thought so. For it was by *faith* that he offered to God a better sacrifice than Cain.

Noah thought so. For it was by *faith* that he prepared the ark, condemned the world, and became the new father of the human race.

Abraham thought so. For it was by *faith* that he journeyed to a promised land, not knowing where he was going. And it was by *faith* that he was also willing to offer up his only begotten son, Isaac.

Moses thought so. For it was by *faith* that he forsook the power, prestige, and pleasures of Egypt.

David thought so. For it was by *faith* that he slew the Giant man called Goliath with a mere sling shot, and later lead a nation to God.

Daniel thought so. For it was by *faith* that he knelt and prayed and gave thanks to God three times a day despite the King's decree against praying, and despite the fact that by breaking the new law that he would suffer the fate of the lion's den.

Job thought so. For it was by *faith* that he held his integrity and did not curse God despite all his afflictions and sorrows.

The apostles thought so. For it was by *faith* that they gave up all that they owned and followed after Jesus.

Jesus thought so. For it was by *faith* that he lived and died and lives again by the words of the Living God!

The Founding Fathers of America thought so. For it was by *faith* that those fifty-six men signed their names to the document that would either bring about freedom for all the colonists *or* would bring about death (by hanging) for the fifty-six!

All these men, and many more like them have lived and died with the hope that something better exists. That *something* is heaven and a paradise earth under a one-world government with Christ as its King.

I believe that Dr. D. James Kennedy aptly put this issue of faith into perspective in his book *Messiah: Prophecies Fulfilled* when he stated "Our trust in the Bible, God, and Jesus is not built upon fantasies and hopes, but on facts...To be a realist, one must be a Christian, for only in the teachings of the Christian faith can a person find a consistent and rational explanation of the world in which we live."

The good news is that because the trumpets are now being sounded, many more today (than in recent years gone by) are getting involved, and are standing up for their God-given rights as citizens of a Christian-founded nation. Those who are really meditating upon the Word of God cannot help but to become addicted to its wonderful truth. But Oh what a marvelous addiction to have! And those addicted to God's word *cannot* sit idly by on the fence post and watch as our nation; *our America* sinks lower and lower into the depths of depravity.

When I think about our situation in view of the Big Picture, I think about the haste that all too many people have today to rush into sin, and I am reminded of the story of the race between the tortoise and the hare. Those who are living after their lust for the flesh, like the rabbit in the story, rush pass the saints, whom are like the turtle. The "rabbits" think they are wiser; they think that they are really getting somewhere fast. They even ridicule and make fun of the slower, more cautious, conservative "turtles." But the saints, like the tortoise, just keep prodding along, keeping their faith, waiting patiently for a better world to come.... For the saints, the future is a better tale to tell and a better song to sing, for it contains rewards in a world in which sickness, sorrow, and death are things of the past. But for the sinners, woe to them because of offenses...for they should fear not people who can kill the body, but not the soul, but rather fear Him who can kill *both* in hell forevermore.

Chapter Eight

OVERCOMING DEATH

Through Reconciliation

*Forasmuch as the children are partakers of flesh
and blood, he also himself likewise took part of the
same; that through death he might destroy him that
had the power of death, that is, the devil: And deliver
them who through fear of death were all their lifetime
subject to bondage.*

MOST PEOPLE LIVE THEIR ENTIRE LIFETIME WITH the fear that some day the grim reaper will come knocking at their door, and when they answer it, he will take them out and shove them down into a hole in the ground where they will become nothing more than food for worms! They believe that on that fateful day, they will perish and cease to exist *forevermore*.

It is because of this very belief that so many people live much of their lives in frustration, fear, anxiety, and depression. Since they believe that all they have is here and now, they tend to live only for the pleasures of today. Many do so without regards to how their actions affect those around them. "I'm going to get all I can during this one brief moment I have here on Earth before it's too late." is there motto. Their idea of happiness is "Me and

Mine first (and foremost) regardless of how the lifestyles of Me and Mine affect you and yours." And so it is with those who place little, if any restraints on their urges for the lust of the flesh.

So how are people of faith different? Because they *do* live their lives with regards to the life hereafter. They *do* believe that how they behave here and now...will have consequences later on.

Many Infallible Proofs

Many people in the gay communities are sick—they are dying—and it is a sad and tragic thing. It is sad because they are dying needlessly. And they are dying needlessly because they have been *deceived*. They have been, as the Bible says, *afflicted*. Because God resists the proud, he tells the double minded to "Be afflicted, and mourn, and weep: let your laughter be turned to mourning, and your joy to heaviness." {James 4:9}. Indeed, the laughter of those who have contracted AIDS (due to their sexual promiscuity) has been turned to mourning, and their joy has been turned to heaviness.

When faced with their own mortality, some of these people have undoubtedly asked the question "Why do the followers of Christ believe that there is actually a life *after* death? And the answers given to that question are limited only by a person's lack of faith, lack of understanding, and lack of knowledge of the world around them. But by doing some research, anybody who is interested in this topic (life *after* death) can be truly enlightened by what they find. The good lawyer, who proves his case in court, is the one who painstakingly attempts to find much in the way of evidence. Like trying to build a puzzle by finding the right pieces, he builds his case by mounting the evidence. With this in mind, the author has included some of the many pieces to the puzzle (reasons that the Christian believes) in life after death.

theism

The belief that God *is* God, and that His words are truth personified.

bible accuracy

The belief that all the Scriptures are God-breathed, just as they claim to be. Note: "All scripture is given by inspiration of God, and is profitable for doctrine (teaching) for reproof, for correction, for instruction in righteousness." {2Timothy 3:16}. Also see: {Jeremiah 1:4, Luke 11:51, 17:26-33, 1Corinthians 2:13, 1Thessalonians 2:13 and 2Peter 3:16}.

bible unity

The Bible is truly one of a kind. It was written over a fifteen hundred year span, in three different languages, by some forty different writers, who represented some twenty different occupations, while living in ten different countries! And yet this book runs together smoothly, in perfect working order, and without contradiction! Upon close examination, we find that the different passages of Scripture not only agree with one another, but that they also actually support and clarify each other's meanings. No book written by man over such a long period of time and by so many different writers could come out as perfect as the Bible has without having been inspired by a Higher Power.

pre-existing knowledge

The Bible contains information that was written "before its time." The writers of the Bible describe all manners of processes, procedures, facts, and figures that they could not have known about (at their point in history) unless they were inspired by an Omniscient Being. Examples of these can be found in our modern day studies of the sciences.

It is ironical today that those who profess that science and the Bible are incompatible are the same people whose very study of the sciences was given *to* them *by* those who believed in the Bible! The foundations of nearly all of our modern sciences were laid out by those who saw the evidence in science as proof of the authenticity of the Scriptures. Names such as Newton, Faraday, Maxwell, Pascal, Boyle, Franklin, Maury, Ray, Simpson, and Strutt are some examples, and there are many, many more.

astronomy

From their eyewitnessing of the planets, the stars, and the earth, the Christian sees evidence of the handiwork of a Creator God. From the movement of the celestial bodies to the rising and setting of the sun, to all the other perfectly balanced processes that take place in nature, and that sustain human life on *this* planet and no others, the Christian sees how these very things are kept in order by the Grand Architect of nature itself.

Take Johann Kepler, the founder of physical astronomy, for example. He not only discovered the laws that govern planetary motion and proved the heliocentric nature of the solar system (all planets revolving around the sun), but he also published the ephemeris tables that were necessary for plotting star movement, thus contributing to the theory of calculus. Possessing great intellect, Kepler once said this: "We astronomers say, with the common people, the planets stand still or go down; the sun rises or sets. How much less should we require than the Scriptures of Divine inspiration, setting aside the common mode of speech, should shape their words according to the model of the natural scientist, and, by employing a dark and inappropriate phraseology about things which surpass the comprehension of those whom it designs to instruct, perplex the people of God, and thus obstruct its own way towards the attainment of the far more exalted object at which it aims."

Pretty deep stuff, wouldn't you say? To comprehend its full meaning, most of us would do well to read the aforementioned statement more than once.

Wernher von Braun, another great intellectual, was the director of NASA and the U.S. guided missile program, and one of the top space scientists in the world. He even became known as the "Father of the American Space Program." Did this great scientist, who knew so much about the vast reaches of outer space, say that mankind originated by mere chance? Far from it! Instead, he said this: "They (the evolutionists) challenge science to prove the existence of God. But must we really light a candle to see the sun?" He also said: "It is in scientific honesty that I endorse the presentation of alternative theories for the origin of the universe, life and man in the science classroom. It would be an error to overlook the possibility that the universe was planned rather than happening by chance."

The Father of the American Space Program said this as well: "In this age of space flight, when we use the modern tools of science to advance into new regions of human activity, the Bible remains in every way an up-to-date book." And he went on to say: "Manned space flight is an amazing achievement, but it has opened for mankind thus far only a tiny door for viewing the awesome reaches of space. An outlook through this peephole at the vast mysteries of the universe should only confirm our belief in the certainty of its Creator."

The Bible itself describes the handiwork of God in many of its passages. Some seven hundred years before Christ, the prophet Isaiah said that God "sitteth upon the circle of the earth"{Isaiah 40:22}, revealing that the earth was round even though "civilized man" thought it to be flat until around twenty-two hundred years later!

In the book of Job, we read how God inspired the writer to say "God hangeth the earth upon nothing in empty space." {Job 26:7}. We now know the earth rotates on its axis and our astronauts have photographed this beautiful sphere, but the people of Job's day could not have looked into outer space to see a view of how the earth "hangeth upon nothing."

meteorology

The prophets of the books of Ecclesiastes and Job described atmospheric circulation. In Ecclesiastes, the prophet describes how "the wind goes toward the south, and turns about unto the north, it whirls about continually, and it returns again according to *his* circuits." {Ecclesiastes 1:6}. And in the book of Job, we find the mention of how God made the winds have weight to them. {Job 28:25}. When these two facts are combined, we can now see that these writers described the very process by which atmospheric circulation takes place (as described in our modern science of meteorology). They did so thousands of years before our modern scientists laid claim to it, and they did so in words that people of their day as well as people of today could understand.

environmental science

The prophet of Ecclesiastes also posed a question "Is there anything whereof it may be said, See this is new?" And then he answered his own question. "It has been already of old time, which was before us." {Ecclesiastes 1:10}.

Most of our modern day inventors are, in truth, merely repackaging that which has already been observed in nature. For example, men studied the rows of flaps of feathers on birds' wings to design airplane wings. Experiments show that birds, bees, dolphins, and many other living organisms had been using internal magnetic compasses long before man had "invented" one. Wasps, yellow jackets, and hornets produced paper for their nests by chewing up weathered wood long before people realized a need for the uses of paper. The process of air conditioning was in use by termites long before man had thought of it. Before man had invented clocks to tell time, microscopic plants known as diatoms were using their internal clocks to tell time. Fiddler crabs, birds, and other animals are also now known to be able to tell time *accurately*. Around five hundred different varieties of fish have internal batteries that produce electricity. They were using their batteries long before Edison came on the scene. Bats were using sonar way before man ever conceived of the idea. Thermometers, submarines, the rotary engine, incubators, jet propulsion, farming, lighting, navigation, medicines, etc...all were being used by living organisms such as crabs, ants, birds, lightning bugs, and others...long before man realized that he too could put these things that are found in nature (that were created by the Lord of Hosts) to good use.

medical science

Louis Pasteur was the famous French scientist who developed the process of "Pasteurization" for milk. He also developed the vaccines for anthrax, chicken cholera, and rabies. As a physicist and chemist, he revolutionized the medical field by establishing the germ theory of disease, organic basis and regulation of fermentation, and bacteriology. This man's research laid the foundation for the control of tuberculosis, diphtheria, tetanus, and many other diseases.

Pasteur denounced evolution. He said "Microscopic beings must come into the world from parents similar to themselves." He also said "The more I study nature, the more I stand amazed at the work of the Creator." In speaking of science, Pasteur said simply this: "Science brings man nearer to God."

The Bible not only lists cures for sickness and disease, it also tells us how to prevent them in the first place. For example:

*STD's. The sexual procedures that God instructed people to avoid in the books of Leviticus, Romans, and Corinthians were designed not only to keep people from sin, but also to protect them from serious physical and mental ailments. Today these ailments are called sexually transmitted diseases, and include but are not limited to sterility, miscarriages, birth defects, brain damage, heart trouble, arthritis, paralyses, insanity, deafness, decomposition, and even death.

*Eighth day circumcision. The procedure for circumcising a male baby on the eighth day of it's life as the Lord told Moses to instruct the Israelites {see Leviticus 12:3} is, as modern medical science has "discovered" *the single day* that the human body provides its highest level of blood clotting during its *entire* lifetime!

*Sanitation. The procedure for quarantine to stop leprosy (that was also described in the book of Leviticus) was used by the European nations during the 14th century to stop the plague of Black Death, which took the lives of around twenty-five percent of their population. When all else had failed, they finally turned to the Scriptures and found the answer!

other sciences

That famous American physicist, Albert Einstein, who developed the theory of relativity said "Science without religion is lame; religion without science is blind."

Sir William Thompson, Lord Kelvin, the famous scientist who developed degrees Kelvin to record temperatures on an absolute scale, helped to formulate the First and Second Laws of Thermodynamics, introduced the Concept of Energy, invented the ship's compass, helped to design and lay the first transatlantic telegraph cable, and had twenty-one honorary degrees awarded to his name, had these things to say regarding the relationship between science and religion: "...science positively affirms creative power." and "...physical science absolutely demonstrates the scientific truth of the (scriptures)." Kelvin, also a university professor, opened each of his lectures with prayer.

George Washington Carver, the agricultural chemist who revolutionized the economy of the south by discovering hundreds of uses for the peanut, soybean, sweet potato and more, became a confidant and advisor to leaders and scientists from all over the world. He was associated with men the likes of Thomas Edison, Henry Ford, Booker T. Washington and even Mahatma Gandhi. Carver said this: "As I worked on projects which fulfilled a real human need, forces were working through me which amazed me. I would often go to sleep with an apparently insoluble problem. When I woke, the answer was there. Why, then, should we who believe in Christ be so surprised at what God can do with a willing man in a laboratory? Some things must be baffling to the critic who has never been born again."

In speaking of nature, Carver said: "I love to think of nature as an unlimited broadcasting station through which God speaks to us every hour, if we will only tune in." He also said: "By nature I am a conserver. I have found nature to be a conserver. Nothing is wasted or permanently lost in nature. Things change their form, but they do not cease to exist. After leaving this world, I do not believe that I am through...When you get your grip on the last rung of the ladder and look over the wall as I am now doing, you don't need their proofs. You see. You know you will not die."

reproduction

With all the technology available today, we know that never once in all of recorded history has any human mother given birth to anything other than a human baby. The same holds true for animals. All species reproduce "after their kinds" just as the Bible has been telling us for thousands of years. A white mother may give birth to a half-black baby, but it's still a *human* baby. A dog may give birth to a mixed breed of dog, but it never gives birth to anything *other than* a dog. This is what is meant by the true meaning of *variations*.

extinction

The knowledge that many different species of animals are becoming extinct with each passing year, which is just the *opposite* of the formation of *new* types of animals (as one would expect to see from evolution) should be a wake up call to even the most skeptical of scientists *if* they have an open mind and study the evidence in search of the *facts*, as scientists are supposed to do.

the fossil record

In response to the media's attempts to push their godless viewpoints on society, more and more concerned Christian scientists are getting the true word of creationism out. The fossil record reveals the rapid burial of all manners of life forms— giving convincing proof of the great deluge that is described in the very first book of the Holy Bible.

archaeology

Through the research and excavation of ancient Palestine, American clergyman and biblical scholar, Edward Robinson published *Biblical Researches in Palestine* in 1841. It was his findings that paved the way for other scholars to follow. By the early 1900's American, French, and German archaeological teams began excavations in Palestine primarily to find the remains of the ancient cities that are mentioned in the Bible. During and since that time, archaeological finds such as those found in the region of the Fertile Crescent confirm the historical accuracy of the words that are written in the Scriptures. Some intriguing examples include:

*An aqueduct and theater of King Herod in Caesarea, an ancient city of Palestine. Excavations there between 1950 and 1961 unearthed the main features of the city as described by the

First-Century historian, Josephus. Included in the find was an inscription of Pontius Pilate!

*The clay prism of Assyrian King Sennacherib's own account of his invasion of Judah in Jerusalem (the account of the invasion is described in the Bible in the books of Second Kings and Second Chronicles).

*Five of the fifteen great gates of Sennacherib's city wall in Nineveh (the capital of ancient Assyria) have been excavated. Twenty-five miles from the city, in Jerwan, sections of an aqueduct built by the king still stand.

*The palaces of both Sennacherib and his grandson, Ashurbanipal, have been found at Kuyunjik. Sennacherib's palace had at least eighty rooms. The throne room which contained bas-reliefs depicting scenes of conquest have now been partially restored.

*When it comes to ancient inscriptions, the library of Ashurbanipal is an unrivaled source for our current day understanding of Mesopotamian history. In all, excavations have unearthed more than *twenty thousand* cuneiform tablets and fragments including the writings of dictionaries, religious matters, and the sciences!

Other historical finds include:

*Babylonian historical texts describing Nebuchadnezzar's conquest of Jerusalem.

*Stables in Megiddo where King Solomon's chariot horses were kept.

*Ancient Hebrew script written on pottery known as the Lachish Letters, which contain writings from military personnel who were engaged in the Babylonian siege itself!

*The remains of a Hittite city confirming the existence of the ancient Hittites (which many scholars believed never existed).

*Evidence of the ruins of the ancient cities of Sodom and Nineveh.

*The famous Dead Sea Scrolls which were discovered in 1947 in the Judean wilderness, as well as fragments of other scrolls discovered at Masada.

*In the valley of the Kings in western Thebes, Egypt, the

tombs and bones of some of the many sons of Ramses II have recently been unearthed. A recent TV documentary with TV anchorman, Hugh Downs, who interviewed some of the archaeologists involved in the dig in Cairo, showed the elaborate tombs, bones, and the actual mummified corpse of Ramses himself!

*The tomb of Seti I (the father of Ramses) has been discovered as well.

*It has now come to light that the actual remains of the ark of Noah may indeed be located on the mountains of Ararat in modern day Turkey! This is the very location that the book of Genesis says that the ark landed after the flood. Many people of good reputation (and with nothing to gain by lying), have come forth with their eyewitness accounts of the ark. Even James Irwin, the former US astronaut who operated the first Lunar Rover vehicle in 1971, and was the eighth man to walk on the moon, claimed to have seen the ark.

It is interesting to note that many ancient writings from other cultures from around the globe (some of which had never had access to the Scriptures of the Holy Bible) depict the account of a worldwide flood and the one family that survived it.

Another interesting thing to note is that some three hundred years prior to their being conquered by the Israelites, the Canaanite civilization occupied Palestine (Canaan). According to records of antiquity, these people (who are mentioned in fifteen different books of the Bible) developed a simplified system of writing. This "system" has ultimately become the basis for all of our modern-day alphabets!

Many records of antiquity by writers (outside of the Bible) have also been found. These writings authenticate the birth, life, persecution, and following of Christ. Roman historians such as Tacitus, Suetonius, Pliny The Younger, and Josephus give references to events centering around one Jesus of Nazareth. The Babylonian Talmud does the same.

If you ever get a chance to visit Cairo (the largest city in Africa) which is located on the eastern bank of the Nile River, and is the capital of Egypt, you will find that it houses one of the world's best archaeological collections of distinctive artifacts.

Many of those artifacts give credence to the dates, places, and peoples that are mentioned in the Bible.

complexity

As we look around us at the overwhelming evidence that everything that serves a purpose such as cars, computers, books, airplanes, space probes, the sciences, the arts; (all that we use today, and will use tomorrow) we can see that they have all been created with the backing of intelligent design—which calls for a *designer*. Processes that happen by chance, on the other hand, wreck havoc and produce waste. For example, a tornado ripping through a junkyard does not leave behind a new Rolls Royce formed from the parts!

fulfilled prophecies

Many of the Bible's prophecies have already been fulfilled (as well documented by historical records). According to bible scholars, the Old Testament relates well over three hundred prophecies concerning Jesus. Just a few examples include:

*Some people of Jesus' day knew that some of the Old Testament books referred to the coming of the Messiah. King Herod was so afraid that the prophesied "ruler in Israel" would steal his kingdom, that he had the male infants of the town in which it was prophesied that Jesus would be born (Bethlehem) slaughtered. By doing so, King Herod unknowingly fulfilled yet another prophecy!

*In the seventh chapter of the book of Isaiah, it was prophesied that a virgin would conceive, bear a son, and call his name Immanuel.

*Nearly five hundred years before Christ came, the prophetic vision of sixty-nine weeks was given to the prophet Daniel, and it pinpointed the *exact time* of the coming of the Messiah.

*The fifty-third chapter of Isaiah describes one who is despised and rejected of men: a man of sorrows...who hath borne our griefs, and carried our sorrows...who was wounded for our transgressions, bruised for our iniquities...who bore our sin without complaint...and with who's stripes we are healed. This description of our Saviour was given around seven hundred years before his birth!

*Other Old Testament passages tell how Jesus would be declared to be the son of God, would ride into Jerusalem on a donkey, and would be killed by the people, then resurrected on the third day.

The Old Testament prophets also predicted scores of other events. For example:

*Isaiah spoke about the Persian king Cyrus, and how he would restore the nation of Judah. He wrote this at least eighty years prior to Cyrus becoming king of the Persian Empire.

*The prophet Ezekial declared the *perpetual* destruction of the city of Tyre and the cities of the nation of Edom.

*The prophet Jeremiah warned God's people of the catastrophe that would come upon their nation because of their sin. He lived to see this prophecy fulfilled when Jerusalem fell to the Babylonian king, Nebuchadnezzar.

*Jeremiah predicted the future outcomes of the nations of Egypt, Moab, Ammon, Edom, Elam, Babylonia, and others. He also foresaw the utter destruction of the (once thought to be impregnable) city of Babylon.

*The landscapes *today* of the destruction of the cities of Edom, Tyre, Babylon, and others like them, bear chilling testimony to the accuracy of Bible prophecy as found in detailed descriptions of the eventual outcome of these places. Their predictions were written by the prophets of the Bible more than twenty-five hundred years ago!

In all, over *two thousand* Bible prophecies have already come to pass (as well documented by historical records) that include events centering around the life of the promised Messiah, the rise and fall of cities and nations, the names of kings and leaders, the complete and enduring destruction of some peoples and places, and the reuniting and rebuilding of others, and more.

goodness

The Christian sees proof of the authenticity of the Scriptures (and therefore the soundness of life after death) from the hard physical evidence that is found in archaeology. The Christian sees the proof that has been provided from the fulfilled prophecies of the Scriptures as well. But the true person of faith does not even need these things in order that they may believe, for all they have to do is wake up in the morning and see the sunrise. For the meek at heart, that alone is enough.

Those of faith *see* the things of God. They see, and they understand the goodness that is all around them. They see goodness in the blessed life-long union of holy matrimony and those things that come with it. Things such as the love they share, the holding in one's arms of a helpless little baby for the first time, the smiles, the laughter, the playing of the young children as they grow and learn, the loving kindness of a father's instruction, and the nurturing love of a warm-hearted mother...

They see goodness in nature such as the beauty of the twinkling stars on a moon-lit night, the magnificent array of colors of the trees on an autumn day, the splendor of the flower budding in the springtime, the glistening crystal dewdrops that rest gently upon the flower's pedals, the ever-flowing current of a brook, the early morning singing of the birds, the chirping of the crickets in the evening...

They see goodness in the wide assortment of foods that grow from the ground, and the wide variety of smells and flavors that they provide...

They see goodness in the fresh air we breathe...

They see how all these things, and many more like them, cannot be the results of chaos or an environment that is the result of random chance. Far from it! No, the Christian *knows* that these things are gifts from God. As the Scriptures state: "Every good and perfect gift is from above, coming down from the Father of heavenly lights." {James 1:17}.

evil

But the evidence of the goodness of God is not all that followers of Christ see. They also notice the discord around them. The Bible offends those who choose to live a life of sin when it explains the future judgment for those who stay the wrongful course. People of faith see how the unsaved live and behave. Not only do the unsaved reject the teachings of the Bible, but they also try to disprove its claims. People of faith see these very things that the Bible describes as "evil" happening all around them, and they know that these things must come to pass in order for man to realize his need for God to come back and set up his Great Government of peace and harmony on earth, for man has failed miserably in his attempts to do so.

persecution

The persecution of Christians has been occurring for nearly two thousand years now. In this past century alone, it has been estimated that more Christians have been persecuted because of their faith than in all the previous centuries combined! The followers of Christ know that this stepping up of the persecution of Christians in our modern "civilized" world was also foretold in the pages of the Holy Bible as a sign of the end days.

forgiveness

People who come to a knowledge of God's forgiveness and mercy realize that they too need to forgive others around them. Then they begin to live a new life; one no longer enslaved by regrets over past sins, and no longer cluttered up with hateful resentment toward others. This too serves as proof of what the Bible says on this very matter.

longevity

The Christian sees how God lets people live only as long as he wishes them to do so. Before mankind became filled with violence and corrupt before God, man lived several hundred years. The Bible gives the ages of men who even lived to be over nine hundred years old! But God said since man was flesh (corruptible), that His spirit would not always strive with man. So for this life, God limited man's age to the maximum of one hundred and twenty years. {Genesis 6:3}.

death

Christians see how death comes to all because of sin. They

notice how nothing of this world; no amount of power, fame, or fortune can save the person whose "time has come."

desire

The *desire* that is built into all people for existence *after* death—where did it come from? The Christian knows. If it were not imparted to us by an all-wise Creator, then why would we have the desire in the first place?

resurrection

The Christian sees how the rose that dies and is buried far beneath the falling snow of winter, comes back to life again in the spring. And thus, he sees proof of the resurrection within resurrection itself!

wisdom

Followers of Christ know that happiness, patience, peace of mind, and serenity all come to those who read the Bible and pray to God.

And the list goes on and on...

As one can see, there is indeed much in the way of solid evidence that points to the many infallible proofs of Bible accuracy. Indeed, the Bible stands on its own authority, just as it claims to do. And since God's word declares that he has the power over both life and death, *this* then is the reason why the Christian believes in life *after* death.

The Spirit That Overcomes Death

Indeed, is there life after death??? This is the all-intriguing question of people that have lived and died down through the ages. The word of God says there *is*. The New Testament not only declares it—it emphasizes it! "The Father raiseth up the dead and gives power to the Son to do the same." {See John 5:21-29, Romans 8:10-14, and I Corinthians 15:51-54}.

One day, the author watched as a young child playing with a

toy ice cream truck stopped, picked up the toy, and proceeded to uncover the battery case, and remove its batteries. And of course the toy could no longer travel back and forth, flash its bright lights on and off, or make the sounds of "Ice cream...Ice cream!" When the child did this, it occurred to the author that our lives are pretty much the same as that little toy, or any device that requires a power source for that matter. Without a power source, we too cannot function. After death, only God can restore our "batteries" and enable us to function once again, for only HE holds the key to the power source for each and every one of our lives.

The apostles spoke about this spirit that overcomes death. The apostle Peter, while filled with the Holy Ghost, declared emphatically that Jesus holds the key to life after death, and that there is salvation in none other for there is no other name under heaven by which we must be saved.

The apostle Paul stated that "The wages of sin is death, but the gift of God is eternal life *through* Jesus Christ, our Lord." In his first letter to the Church of God at Corinth, Paul clearly describes the Resurrection of Life in the fifteenth chapter. At the end of his life, Paul also said "...there is laid up for me a crown of righteousness, which the Lord, the righteous judge, shall give me: and not to me only, but to all who love his appearing."

Not only did the apostles of the New Testament proclaim the good news of the Resurrection {See Acts 1:3}, but in the Old Testament many servants of God, such as Abraham, for one, spoke about the Resurrection as well. The final book of the Bible, the Revelation *confirms* the Resurrection. {Revelation 1:18}.

Nine Were Raised—Two *Never* Died!

In the pages of the Holy Bible, the inspired and infallible word of the Living God, we find that not only were Lazarus and Jesus raised from death, but many others were as well! The Old Testament books of Kings give the accounts of God's prophets Elijah and Elisha who, when imparted with God's power each restored the lives of a child. Also, the body of a man who had died was lowered into the sepulcher of Elisha. When it touched

Elisha's bones, the man revived and stood up!

Nearly everyone has heard of the account of Lazarus. Jesus called him forth from the grave after he had been dead for four days. But how many know that Jesus also restored the lives of the widow of Nain's son and the daughter of Jairus? And how many are aware that when Jesus yielded up the ghost on the cross, that the graves were opened and many bodies of the saints which slept, arose? They came out of their graves after his resurrection, and went into the holy city, and appeared there to many!

After Christ ascended back up to heaven, his apostle Peter resurrected a woman named Tabitha, and Paul resurrected a young man named Eutychus. Thus the Bible gives the accounts of at least nine people (not counting the risen saints) who literally died, and then came back to life—through the power of the living God!

It is also interesting to note that the Bible gives the accounts of Enoch and Elijah *who never died!* The seventh from Adam, Enoch lived 365 years and then God *translated* him because he was a man who walked with God, and he pleased Him. Written about in the books of Genesis, Hebrews, and Jude, this man's life is an amazing testimony to the power God has of life over death and his faithfulness toward those who walk in his ways.

Elijah also walked in the path of righteousness, and while speaking with Elisha, a chariot of fire appeared, and then Elijah went up by a whirlwind into heaven. His story is related to us in Second Kings.

Before reading this book, perhaps many of you were not aware that some of the aforementioned things are related to us in God's holy word. But the prophet Isaiah said that those who are made to understand doctrine must learn it "precept upon precept, precept upon precept; line upon line, line upon line; here a little, and there a little." {See Isaiah 28:10 and 28:13}.

Why The Early Christians Endured

Should not those who profess to be atheists be inclined to wonder why a handful of early Christians endured long enough for their Christian faith to not only survive in a wicked world, even to this very day, but to also become the largest Church following that has *ever* existed? The early Christians did not have the advantages of modern technology such as TV, radio, or the advances that have been made in the sciences to prove or disprove things the way we can today. But they did have *many infallible proofs* {Acts 1:3}, and they had eyewitness accounts. They had their own *experience.* What they saw enabled them to endure all the attempts of the government, the "religious" leaders of the day, and other enemies of Christ to silence the movement at its very onset. They began to preach the good news of Christ's mission (the gospel) despite the constant persecution that they faced for doing so. Day after day, month after month, and year after year they were persecuted. *But they did not stop!*

The Bible itself tells us why the early followers of Christ endured all manners of evil against them. In the eleventh chapter of the Gospel of Saint John, we read one of the most intriguing and exciting statements of the entire Bible. There, Jesus said that some people will *never* die! Four days after Lazarus had died, Jesus arrived at the place where the people had buried him. Lazarus' sister Martha approached Jesus and said that if he had been there, that her brother would not have died. Then, Jesus said unto her "I am the resurrection, and the life: he that believeth in me, though he were dead, yet shall he live: And whosoever liveth and believeth in me shall never die."{John 11:25-26}. What an incredible statement! I believe that here, Jesus was saying that his second coming is not only an actual event that is going to take place, but at that very time, those that are following after him will be, as Enoch and Elijah were (transformed), and shall *never* die!

In the book of the Acts of the Apostles, in the first and second chapters, we read that before he was taken up to heaven, Jesus gave instructions to his apostles. For forty days after his death, he appeared to them many times in ways that proved beyond a shadow of a doubt that he was no mere ghost, but rather a living, breathing, heart-beating, red-blooded man who was very much *alive.* At one point during this time, he appeared to five hundred of his followers! {1 Corinthians 15:6}. He told some of them to wait for the gift of the Holy Spirit, which would come upon them. Christ then ascended up into heaven right before their eyes. As they stood there gazing up into heaven, two men dressed in white appeared to them and told them not to marvel for one day Jesus would return in like manner. {Acts 1:9-11}.

On the day of Pentecost, the Holy Spirit came upon the apostles and enabled them to speak different languages. So they began an amazing quest to preach the word of peace by Jesus Christ to the nations. They preached how God had anointed Jesus of Nazareth with the Holy Ghost and with power. They preached how he went about doing good and healing all that were oppressed of the devil. They preached how they bore witness to all things that he did both in the land of the Jews and in Jerusalem. They preached how the people turned on him and had him slain and hung on a tree. They preached how God raised him up on the third day and showed him openly to the witnesses chosen of God. They preached of how he ate and drank with them after he rose from the dead, and how he commanded them to preach to people that it is he which was ordained of God to be the Judge of the quick and the dead. To him gave all the prophets witness, that through his name whosoever believes upon him shall receive remission of sins. {See Acts 10:38-43}.

In the letter that the apostle Paul wrote to the Romans to prepare the way for his visit to the Church at Rome, he said this "Who shall separate us from the love of Christ? Shall tribulation, or distress, or persecution, or famine, or nakedness, or peril, or sword?" {Romans 8:35}. And he went on to say "Nay, in all these things we are more than conquerors through him that loved us. For I am persuaded, that neither death, nor life, nor angels, nor principalities, nor powers, nor things present, nor things to come, nor height, nor depth, nor any other creature shall be able to separate us from the love of God, which is in Christ Jesus our Lord." {Romans 8:37-39}.

Now why would a man, *any man* say such things to uphold anything other than that which he knew to be absolutely true? If these things were not true, he would have had nothing to gain except for pain. The reason he and others like him said these things is clear. It is because Jesus *was* resurrected from the dead as the firstborn of those who will be resurrected to *eternal life!*

These individuals who have been called out among the multitudes are the "elect." Jesus himself even reassured them of this when he said "...I go to prepare a place for you... because I live, you shall live also." {John 14:2, 19}. And he also said "Rejoice and be exceeding glad: for great *is* your reward in heaven: for so persecuted they the prophets which were before you." {Matthew 5:12}.

And so the early followers of Christ endured. They endured with the promise that they would receive unimaginable joy. They were told to be exceedingly glad! They endured because the events that transpired in their day made them come to understand salvation.

Even Torture And Death Did Not Stop Them

Early Christians who had witnessed Christ's miracles, his death, and his teaching after his resurrection, were literally tortured to death because they would not recant their faith to the "powers that be." Records of antiquity bear witness to the accounts of the martyrdom of many of the early followers of the Christian faith. These followers were imprisoned, they were scourged, flogged, beaten, spit on, stoned, bludgeoned, speared, boiled in oil, doused in tar and then set on fire, starved to death, thrown to wild beasts, dragged down steps by a bull, ripped apart on the pulleys, and yes, even crucified. (And these are only *some* of things they endured).

It has been written that Timothy was martyred in Ephesus when he protested the orgies and the idol worship of the goddess Diana (Artemis) that took place there. And it has also been reported that Peter was crucified upside-down because he said he was not worthy to die the same way his Saviour had died! Some of the other apostles experienced similar persecutions. The early Christians endured these and many other unspeakable horrors because they knew that *this* life can not be compared to the *next*!

The early Church also suffered ridicule, criticism, and persecution when they abandoned the celebration of the most significant holy day (holiday) in their nation's history (the Passover) to celebrate Easter instead. Why would they do this?

Because the resurrection of Christ took the place of it. The holy Lamb of God paid the supreme sacrifice once and for all for those who believe, repent, and come to him for salvation.

We now know that from not only the accounts outlined in Scripture, but from other historical records as well, that after Christ's ascension *to this very day*...people have been being persecuted for the cause of Christianity.

Christ's Victory Over Death Can Be *Your* Victory Too!

On October 24, 1852, just a few hours before his death, Daniel Webster slowly said "...What would the condition of any of us be if we had not the hope of immortality?...Thank God, the Gospel of Jesus Christ brought life and immortality to light, rescued it—brought it to light." His last coherent words were "I still live."

Just think about that for a moment. What is it that any of us wants more than anything else at that fateful moment? Will it be more money? No. We won't be able to take it with us to where we are going. Will it be for fame? No. We won't be cognizant of our fame if it occurs after we are dead and gone. Will it be for sex? No. That won't do the trick because we won't have any time left for that. The only thing that we can hope for at that very moment is for *immortality*. Life everlasting in peace and joy is the only thing *worth* hoping for. And if we hope for it, we are not alone by any means.

On May 17, 1829, as he too was approaching death, John Jay was asked if he had any final words for his children, to which he responded: "They have the Book." (He was referring to the Bible.) Jay had these words placed in his Last Will and Testament "Unto Him who is the author and giver of all good, I render sincere and humble thanks for His merciful and unmerited blessings, and especially for our redemption and salvation by his beloved Son."

Andrew Jackson, our seventh president and the man who named the state of Tennessee, wrote in his will "The bible is true. Upon that sacred Volume I rest my hope of eternal salvation through the merits of our blessed Lord and Saviour Jesus Christ." On June 8, 1845, just moments before his death,

Jackson called his family and his servants to his bedside and told them "My dear children, do not grieve for me; it is true, I am going to leave you; I am well aware of my situation. I have suffered much bodily pain, but my sufferings are but as nothing compared with that which our blessed Redeemer endured upon the accursed Cross, that all might be saved who put their trust in Him."

Patrick Henry, the five-time Governor of the State of Virginia who coined the phrase "Give me Liberty or give me death!" wrote in his will "This is all the inheritance I give to my dear family. The religion of Christ will give them one which will make them rich indeed." While he lay dying, Henry said "I am much consoled by reflecting that the religion of Christ has, from its first appearance in the world, been attacked in vain by all the wits, philosophers, and wise ones, aided by every power of man, and its triumphs have been complete."

In the will of the Father of the American Revolution, Sam Adams, it is written: "Principally, and first of all, I resign my soul to the Almighty Being who gave it, and my body I commit to the dust, relying on the merits of Jesus Christ for the pardon of my sins."

George Mason was the famous American Revolutionary statesman and delegate from Virginia to the Constitutional Convention who refused to sign the Constitution because it did not sufficiently limit the government's power from infringing on the rights of citizens. Known as the "Father of the Bill of Rights" he insisted that Congress add the Bill of Rights (the first ten amendments) to the Constitution. Virtually all succeeding constitutions (worldwide) have incorporated the pattern he set forth. Mason, who was also the richest man of his day in the state of Virginia, owned 15,000 acres in that state and some 80,000 acres in the Ohio area. He was also the designer of the Virginia Constitution and the Virginia Bill of Rights. In his will, George Mason wrote "My soul, I resign into the hands of my Almighty Creator, whose tender mercies are over all His works, who hateth nothing that He hath made and to the Justice and Wisdom of whose dispensation I willing and cheerfully submit, humbly hoping from His unbounded mercy and benevolence, through the merits of my blessed Saviour, a remission of my sins."

Charles Dickens, the distinguished author who wrote *Oliver Twist, David Copperfield, Tale of Two Cities*, and *A Christmas Carol,* said in his will "I commit my soul to the mercy of God through our Lord and Saviour Jesus Christ, and I exhort my children to try and guide themselves by the teachings of the New Testament in its broad spirit, and to put no faith in any man's narrow construction of its letter here or there."

William Shakespeare's will says "...I commend my soul into the hands of God, my Creator, hoping and assuredly believing, through the only merits of Jesus Christ, my Saviour, to be made partaker of life everlasting..."

There are many other examples of well known individuals who have, by their very own admission, professed a faith and belief in Christ, which is so very necessary for inheritance into the Kingdom of God and the eternal life hereafter. For the sake of time, I keep the examples listed here few.

Like so many of those believers who came before us, so it is with us also that when we say *O' wretched man that I am, who shall deliver me from this body of death?* We can hear the answer in that quiet place which occupies our innermost thoughts. That place of serenity that does not permit the noises of the outside world to enter in. That still place that seems to carry the answer in on a small breeze that whispers ever so gently those words that our hearts, our minds, and our very souls long to hear...

Jesus Christ will.

It is Christ who lives forever to make intercession for those who place their trust in him! He is that one and only mediator between God and man, and it is through our faith in him that we are restored and he reconciles us *to* God. {See John 14:6}. His shed blood provided us with the only remedy for the disease of sin. And with his death and resurrection he became the *cure* for that dark plague known as *death*. With His victory over death on the cross, Christ has sown the seeds that have become the one true church of the living God. Yes it is Jesus, the Christ, who came into this world to destroy the works of Satan and deliver those who live in fear of dying. It is He who gives us our only hope of assurance, and through that assurance we gain the confidence that overcomes *all* adversity. By placing our faith in Christ, and by letting his power work through us, we can overcome the world by overcoming temptation. And, by the saving grace of God, we can overcome death.

Thy Kingdom Come

When Jesus' followers asked him to teach them how they should pray, he answered them by saying "Pray in this manner...Our Father which art in heaven Hallowed be thy name. Thy Kingdom come. Thy will be done in earth, as it is in heaven. Give us this day our daily bread. And forgive us our debts, as we forgive our debtors. And *lead us not into temptation, but deliver us from evil:* For thine is the Kingdom, and the power, and the glory, forever. Amen." And he went on to say "For if you forgive men their trespasses, your heavenly Father will also forgive you: But if you do not forgive men of their trespasses, neither will your Father forgive your trespasses." {Matthew 6:9-15}. (Emphasis added).

What Jesus was referring to when he said that men should pray "Thy Kingdom come" was that the world's current political-economic system is going to change. Eventually all systems of government by men will fall and be replaced by the Government of God himself! Thus the reason for these words in the prayer.

To better understand the Kingdom of God that will be established upon the earth, we need to look to the book of the Revelation to John. We need to understand that this last book of the Bible was written during that period when the early Christians were being persecuted because of their faith in Jesus as Lord; as the one who delivers from death. Much of the book is written in symbolic language through a series of visions given to John who was most likely the last survivor of the original twelve apostles. John wrote the book around eighty to ninety-five A.D. when he was a prisoner on the Greek island of Patmos, a Roman penal colony for political offenders. Even though much of the wording of the book is symbolic, the message it conveys is clear.

God's fierce anger will be poured out upon the wicked of the earth, and the Second Coming of Christ will usher in a new era in earth history, one unlike any previously. Christ will then set up his Kingdom *here on earth* and he will be the head of the government that will rule over all the inhabitants of this planet. Perhaps this will give a better understanding of the significance of the earth to those who have been fed the Satanic lie of "superior beings on other planets."

In the beginning verses of The Book of Revelation we read these words "Blessed is he who reads, and they that hear the words of this prophesy, and keep those things which are written in it; for the time is at hand." Now bearing in mind that a thousand years is as a day to the Lord, we are currently living in the very end of the second day (since the writing of Revelation). Since the very structure of time that the world uses in reckoning dates is based upon Christ (B.C. = Before Christ, A.D. = anno Domini = *in the year* of our Lord), the year A.D. 2000 ends the *second day* of the year of our Lord, and 2001 ushers in the beginning of the *third day*. So even though there are people in the world today who scoff at the mere mentioning of the second coming of Christ (just as the Bible said there would be—*in the last days*), the time is still coming just the same. This book of the Bible contains an urgent message of repentance for everyone who has lived during these past two thousand years. The message being "Look up, be patient, for the coming of the Lord draweth nigh." {James 5:7-8}.

The Coming Utopia

Under God's Kingdom rule, there will be peace on earth as never before. In the second verse of the ninth chapter of the Old Testament book of Isaiah, the prophet said "The people that walked in darkness have seen a great light: they that dwell in the land of the shadow of death, upon them hath the light shined." A few verses later Isaiah explains that light that releases men from their fear of death by saying "For unto us a child is born, unto us a son is given: and the government shall be upon his shoulder: and his name shall be called Wonderful, Counselor, The mighty God, The everlasting Father, The Prince of Peace.

Of the increase of *his* government and peace *there shall be* no end." He wrote these words some seven hundred and fifty years *before* Christ was born!

Later, in the New Testament when Jesus was ministering to his disciples, they asked him point blank "...what shall be the sign of thy coming, and of the end of the world?" {Matthew 24:3}. And He answered them by describing the events that would lead up to his Second Coming. (Those very events are now coming to pass). Christ then went on to describe the tribulation that will come, and then finally said "And then shall appear the sign of the Son of man in heaven: and then shall all the tribes of the earth mourn, and they shall see the Son of man coming in the clouds of heaven with power and great glory." {Matthew 24:30}.

Moving forward to the last two chapters of the book of Revelation, we find a description of the *new* heavens and *new* earth. (These are also described in the Old Testament book of Isaiah and in the second epistle of Peter.) These books describe the destruction of the present heavens and earth and the creation of the new ones. And the new earth shall be governed from the New Jerusalem; a newly created city which will serve as the headquarters of God Almighty himself!

The New Jerusalem is described as an incredibly vast city (1,400 miles long in each direction) with an exterior wall that stands over two hundred feet high and has twelve gates made of solid pearl! Inside, the city is adorned with precious stones such as topaz, emeralds, and sapphires. The streets are made of pure gold which gives them a transparent appearance. There is no night therein, nor any need of a sun or moon for God's own presence illuminates the magnificent city. Those who are allowed to enter into the city are God's own chosen people. Those who follow the path of wickedness will not be allowed to enter therein. {Revelation 21:10-27}.

The Trees Of Life

During this time of peace on earth and good will toward men, life will be a literal paradise for those who have persevered. It will be a place where the old will be made young again, and the sick will be made well. The paradise garden will be restored and the fullness thereof shall be throughout the land. There shall be an abundance of food for everyone. All the animals will be peaceful. There will be no more crime, wars, or violence of any kind. Hatred, selfishness, envying and strife will be things of the past, and those who keep God's commandments will have the right to the trees of life for they will no longer be barred from them as they have been ever since the first human parents sinned by disobeying their Creator.

Anybody interested in *eternal life in paradise* should read the book of Revelation in its entirety. They should read all of the Bible, for that matter.

Conquering The Deception

Unlike flimsy man who changes with every whim of the currents that flow downstream, the Lord our God changeth not. He said so himself. In the days of Moses, He declared that homosexuality was a sin. It was a sin a hundred years later. It was a sin a thousand years later. It is still a sin today, and it will continue to be a sin tomorrow.

In the book of Revelation, Satan is referred to as he "which deceiveth the whole world." Indeed, Satan and his followers have deceived people from all walks of life into believing the lie that it's okay to engage in same sex perversion. He has deceived groups such as the ACLU. He has deceived our highest ranking government officials, and is now deceiving the educators of our children.

In this day in which we are living, I am reminded of the words that the Apostle Paul wrote in his epistles to the Hebrews and to the Ephesians. He warned the Hebrews to "Take heed lest there be in any of you an evil heart of unbelief, in departing from the living God. But exhort one another daily, while it is called today; lest any of you be hardened through the deceitfulness of sin." {Hebrews 3:13}. He also instructed the Ephesians "That we *henceforth* be no more children, tossed to and fro, and carried about with every wind of doctrine, by the sleight of men, and cunning craftiness, whereby they lie in wait to deceive; But speaking the truth in love, may grow up into him in all things, which is the head, even Christ." {Ephesians 4:14-15}.

My dear friend, the dictionary defines *deception* as the act or practice of imposing upon the credulity of others through dishonesty, fraud, or trickery. It is to lead astray or frustrate by means of underhandedness. It is to MISLEAD. It is to *beguile*. Sound familiar? It is, and always has been the very trump card of Satan (the beguiling serpent) himself! But The Word of God clearly states that evil will not deliver those who practice it.

Conquering The Sin

If you walk away with only one thing from this book let it be this: *Satan deceives many people, who in turn, deceive many more!* In this battle against the principalities of darkness, the followers of Christ must not remain silent concerning the gay rights movement, for it is a movement that promotes a sin; and that sin—when it is fully manifested—will destroy a society. The Bible declares it. History *confirms* it.

Remember that those who deceive others are good at taking words out of context from sources such as the Bible and the Constitution, and using those words to defend or rationalize their misguided behaviors. But they won't be able to deceive those who have read this book, for the words written herein have been *As Straight As An Arrow* —> they have exposed the lies; they have bore witness to the truth!

It has always been a lie of Satan's that there is no punishment for sin. But that is not what the Word of God says in the Holy Bible! So one more time, let us separate truth from error.

Satan himself is going to be punished for his wickedness. Eventually, he will be utterly destroyed. The first and last books of the Bible confirm this. For example, in the book of Genesis, God declared that he would put enmity between the serpent and the woman; between the serpent's seed and the woman's seed. He said that the seed of the woman shall bruise the serpent's head, and the serpent would bruise his heel. {Genesis 3:15}. The serpent is Satan, and he bruised the "heel" of Christ when Christ was put to death on the cross. The book of Revelation, on the other hand, pictures Jesus as he who is sitting upon a white horse and is carrying a bow and wearing a crown. He goes forth conquering, and to conquer. It is *He*, this Lord of Lords, who shall come again and shall "bruise the head" of Satan when Satan is tossed into the lake of fire and brimstone. {Revelation 20:10}. God has even declared this in the very stars themselves! There, Christ is depicted as the figure of the man whose left heel is about to be stung by the scorpion, but whose right heel is about to step on the scorpion's head to crush it. The scorpion or "Scorpio" *is* Satan.

Christ is also depicted as that archer in the sky (in the house of Sagittarius) whose bow is drawn taut, and whose arrow is pointing directly at the heart of the scorpion! With this in mind, we finally begin to see that Christ, like the Father, is the mighty archer who ultimately conquers the devil and sin.

A Sexual Addiction: With Grave Consequences

As we draw near to the end of this writing, it is the author's hope that as a result of reading this, the reader will have gained an understanding that those who have this sexual addiction have been spiritually blinded. They have been deceived into believing the lie that they are trapped in a dungeon of darkness—bound to their lusts of the flesh. It is a materialistic viewpoint of life: one with no light at the end of the tunnel.

Those who purposely rebel against God's Word regarding this matter had better think twice, because their attitude is one that in the end has "grave" consequences. They would do well to remember that, as mentioned earlier, the average life span for those who are living the gay lifestyle is only 42 for men, and only 45 for women.

The Conclusion Of The Matter

Do not let yourself be as those who are blind. They cannot see far off and have forgotten that they have been purged from past sins by Christ's supreme sacrifice. Indeed, to be spiritually minded is life and peace, but to be carnally minded is spiritual blindness, and it is death. If you believe these things, then God has quickened you...*you who were once dead* in trespasses and sins. He has turned you back from your lusts of the flesh; the lasciviousness and uncleanness, which now still works in the children of disobedience and wrath. For he is a God of mercy, as well as a God of judgment. He is gracious and full of compassion as he demonstrated when he sent his only son here to die for us.

God is slow to anger. Not one of us deserves his great mercy for all of us have turned away from him (at some point) and have sinned and fallen short of his glory. But it is according to his abundant mercy that he has begotten us again into a lively hope by the resurrection of Jesus from the dead. And even though he is long-suffering toward us, not willing that any should perish but that all should come to repentance, there is coming a day (let me repeat that) there *is* coming a day...a day when Christ *will* return. On that day, every knee shall bow before him, the virtuous as well as the homosexual. For He is coming to usher in peace, but first to execute judgment upon all that are ungodly for all their ungodly deeds, and for all the hard speeches they have made against him. It therefore behooves us all—by the mercies of God—that we present our bodies a living sacrifice, holy and acceptable to God, which is our reasonable service. We should not be conformed to *this* world; but be instead transformed by the renewing of our minds. Once again, let us hear the conclusion of the whole matter: Fear the Lord and keep his commandments, for this is the whole duty of man. For God shall bring every work into judgment (whether it be good, or whether it be evil) even those things done in secret.

In closing, let me borrow the words of that famous Scottish essayist and historian, Thomas Carlyle, who said *"Of all the acts of man, repentance is the most divine. The greatest of all faults is to be conscious of none."*

The End.

RESOURCES

ORGANIZATIONS DEDICATED TO HELPING INDIVIDUALS, FAMILIES, AND
FRIENDS OF THOSE STRUGGLING WITH SAME SEX ADDICTIONS:

<u>Exodus International</u>
Executive Director: Bob Davies
P.O. Box 77652
Seattle, WA 98177
(206) 784-7799
Website: www.exodusintl.org
Monthly Newsletter: *Update*
Quarterly Newsletter: *The Exodus Standard*
(Through Christ, this non-profit, non-denominational organization has been helping men
and women find a way out of homosexuality since 1976. They provide individuals with a
referral list of qualified member ministries, offer direct support to men and women
pursuing sexual purity, stage an annual conference, and provide valuable resources such
as a free monthly newsletter and a free information packet. Their mailing list is
confidential.)

<u>Kerusso Ministries</u>
President: Michael Johnston
P.O. Box 2399
Newport News, VA 23609
(757) 872-8878
Website: www.Kerusso.org
Radio: *Truth Under Fire*
(The leading independent ministry in the country working to provide a balanced and
Biblical Christian viewpoint on the issue of homosexuality as it relates to ministry and
public policy. Founded in 1989, Kerusso Ministries organizes evangelistic meetings and
seminars, produces the weekly radio broadcast "Truth Under Fire" and coordinates the
National Coming Out of Homosexuality Day Project.)

<u>Love In Action</u>
Founder: Frank Worthen
Director: John Smid
P.O. Box 753307
Memphis, TN 38175
(901) 542-0250
Website: www.loveinaction.org
Publications: *Love In Action*, *Between The Lines*, and *Lifelines*
(This organization proclaims the message of hope and imparts courage to a world facing
homosexuality and its subsequent issues by providing support and counseling to
individuals desiring to break away from homosexual behavior and identity. For more
than twenty-five years they have helped people find freedom in Christ, which is God's
love in action.)

National Association for Research and Therapy of Homosexuality (NARTH)
16633 Ventura Blvd.
Suite 1340
Encino, CA 91436
(818) 789-4440
Website: www.narth.com

Regeneration Ministry
P.O. Box 9830
Baltimore, MD 21284
(410) 661-4337
Newsletter: *Regeneration News*
(Provides a monthly newsletter offering meaningful and helpful articles for men and
women that are trying to overcome the gay lifestyle. Catalogs and reviews Christian
books focused on homosexuality issues.)

ORGANIZATIONS FIGHTING AGAINST THE IMMORALITY AND DECADENCE
BEING PROMOTED BY THE NATIONAL MEDIA:

AmeriVision Communications, Inc.
3141 N.W. Expressway
Suite 101
Oklahoma City, OK 73112-4143
(800) 800-7550 or (800) 510-2201
Website: www.tabehrens.com/utilities/lifeline.htm
Tradename: *LifeLine*
(Formed in 1990, Lifeline is a Christian long-distance telephone service whose primary
function is to offer a complete and thorough option of the major long distance carriers'
line of products at a lower price to the consumer while assuring quality service. Lifeline
offers support to Christian ministries and supports pro-family issues while taking a stand
against abortion, the homosexual lifestyle, and sex and violence on television. They
provide a chart listing certain causes that the "Big Three" long distance carriers are
supporting and funding such as pornography, special rights for homosexuals, abortion,
liberal causes and candidates, and sex, violence, and profanity on television.)

Coral Ridge Ministries
President: D. James Kennedy
P.O. Box 40
Ft. Lauderdale, FL 33302
(305) 772-0404
Website: www.coralridge.org
TV: *The Coral Ridge Hour*
Radio: *Truths That Transform*
Newsletter: *Impact*
(Dr. Kennedy is one of the leading Christian statesmen of our time. His Evangelism
Explosion is reaching more and more people for Christ daily.)

Enough Is Enough
President Emeritus: Dee Jepsen
President: Bruce Watson
P.O. Box 888

Fairfax, VA 22030
(703) 278-8343
TV: *Internet Predator* and *Jason*
(A non-partisan, non-profit organization dedicated to addressing the issues of sexual exploitation and illegal pornography. Enough Is Enough stands for a media culture in which people are respected and valued, healthy sexuality; childhood with a protected period of innocence, and a society free from the exploitation of children and women in the name of individual freedom. They also stand for freedom of speech as defined by the Constitution of the United States of America, and the Supreme Court rulings that both obscenity and child pornography are outside the protection of the First Amendment. Their mission is to educate the public about the existence, availability, and dangers of illegal pornography, thereby enlisting public support to make pornographic material unavailable to children, to make illegal pornography unavailable in the marketplace, and to encourage community efforts to guard against illegal pornography and treat its victims.)

Mastermedia International
Chairman: Dr. Larry W. Poland
330 N. Sixth Street
Suite 110
Redlands, CA 92374-3312
(909) 335-7353
Website: www.mastermediaintl.com
Radio: *The Mediator Broadcast*
Newsletter: *The Mediator*
(A non-profit organization that operates Christian ministries to media leaders, primarily in film and television, and seeks to create awareness of the impact of media on individuals, the family, the Church, and society.)

United News and Information
P.O. Box 92311
Pasadena, CA 91109
(202) 783-91109
Radio: *United News and Information*
Newsletter: *Focus*
(World events from a Christian perspective.)

ORGANIZATIONS FIGHTING FOR THE RIGHTS AND VALUES OF THE TRADITIONAL FAMILY IN AMERICA:

Center for Christian Statesmanship
Director: Dr. Frank Wright
214 Massachusetts Avenue, NE
Suite 220
Washington, D.C. 20002
(202) 547-3052
Website: www.statesman.org
Newsletter: *The Statesmanship Statute*
Prayer Bulletin: *Washington Prayer Bulletin*
(Ministers to members on Capitol Hill and keeps citizens aware of decisions in Washington that affect the moral state of the nation.)

<u>The Center For Reclaiming America</u>
National Director: Janet Folger
P.O. Box 632
Ft. Lauderdale, FL 33302
(954) 772-0377 Ext. 622
Website: www.reclaimamerica.org
(A grass-roots network for Christians who wish to make a change in the declining moral
state of our nation. Provides an up to the moment look at news that affects the moral
state of the nation. Provides members with a Christian Alert Bulletin, a telephone
hotline, and more.)

<u>Christian Coalition</u>
President: Don Hodel
P.O. Box 1990
Chesapeake, VA 23327
Website: www.cc.org
(A 1.7 million member grassroots organization that provides America's 40 Million
Christian voters with pertinent information and knowledge they need to make sure their
voices are heard in government. Provides Congressional Scorecards on how *your*
congressman and senators voted on issues critical to the American family.)

<u>Christian Policy Research Institute</u>
Executive Director: Terry Moffitt
P.O. Box 451
High Point, NC 27260
(910) 869-6280
(Studies legislation and its effects on the Christian Community. Provides educational,
political, and ministry consulting services.)

<u>Concerned Women for America</u> (CWA)
Chairman: Beverly LaHaye
1015 Fifteenth Street N.W.
Suite 1100
Washington, D.C. 20005
(202) 488-7000
Website: www.cwfa.org
Radio: *Beverly LaHaye Live*
Magazine: *Family Voice*
(The nation's largest politically active pro-family woman's organization dedicated to
preserving and protecting Judeo-Christian values through educational and legislative
programs.)

<u>Eagle Forum</u>
President: Phyllis Schlafly
P.O. Box 618
Alton, IL 62002
(618) 462-5415
Website: www.eagleforum.org
Radio: *The Phyllis Schlafly Report* & *Phyllis Schlafly Live*
Newsletter: *The Phyllis Schlafly Report* and *Education Reporter*
(Eagle Forum has an office on Capitol Hill that supports conservative and pro-family
policies at every level of government. They stand for the fundamental rights of parents to

guide the education of their children which includes the right to choose private or home schooling. Their mission is to enable conservatives to participate in the process of self-government and public policy-making so that America will continue to be a land of individual liberty with respect for family integrity.)

<u>Family Research Council</u> (FRC)
Executive Vice President and Chief Executive Officer: Chuck Donovan
801 G Street, NW
Washington, D.C. 20001
(202) 393-2100
Website: www.frc.org
Radio: *Family Research Council* & *Washington Watch*
Newsletter: *Washington Watch*
(FRC works diligently to communicate to policy-makers and citizens alike the importance of the strength of the traditional family and the Judeo-Christian principles upon which it is built. Headed up by Gary Bauer for ten years (until he threw his bid in for US presidential candidacy), this organization promotes and defends traditional family values in print, broadcast and other media outlets. It develops and advocates legislative and public policy initiatives to strengthen and fortify the family and promote traditional values. It establishes and maintains accurate statistical and research data that reaffirms the importance of the family in our civilization. It also informs and educates citizens on how they can promote Biblical principles in our culture.)

<u>Focus on the Family</u>
President: Dr. James Dobson
8685 Explorer Drive
Colorado Springs, CO 80920
(719) 531-5181
Website: www.family.org
TV: *Focus on the Family Commentary* (90-second news insert)
Radio: *Focus on the Family* and *Adventures in Odyssey*
Magazine: *Focus on the Family*
Newsletter: *Family News From Focus on the Family*
(Has over 70 outreaches in America, and ministries in over 75 countries worldwide.)

<u>The Institute on Religion and Democracy</u> (IRD)
1521 16th Street, N.W.
Suite 300
Washington, D.C. 20036
(202) 986-1440
Newsletter Magazine: *Faith & Freedom*
(Dedicated to monitoring denominational agencies and leaders and combating radical ideologies such as extremist feminism and liberation theology.)

<u>International Christian Media</u>
President: Marlin Maddoux
P.O. Box 30
Dallas, TX 75221
(800) 227-1444
Website: www.icmc.org
Radio: *Point of View*
(Radio program reaches some 3 million listeners each week over 300 stations nationwide.

Aims to restore the greatness of Christian thought and values to every area of American life by strengthening, informing, training, and mobilizing Christians with well-articulated Christian principles.)

National Association of Evangelicals (NAE)
Vice-President: Robert P. Dugan Jr.
1023 15th Street N.W.
Suite 500
Washington, D.C. 20005
(202) 789-1011
Website: www.nae.net
Newsletter: *NAE Washington Insight*
(Office of Public Affairs made up of professional men and women dedicated to work, watch, and witness for evangelical Christians in their relationship to federal government.)

Religious Freedom Coalition
Chairman: William J. Murray (Son of Madalyn Murray O'Hair)
P.O. Box 77511
Washington, D.C. 20013
(202) 554-2358
Website: www.rfcnet.org
Newsletter: *William J. Murray Report*
(A political action committee supporting candidates who stand for traditional family values and limited governmental control.)

The Urban Alternative
President: Dr. Tony Evans
P.O. Box 4000
Dallas, TX 75208
(214) 943-3868
Website: www.tonyevans.org
TV: *The Alternative*
Radio: *The Alternative*
(Dr. Evans, who aggressively promotes the rebuilding of our cities from the inside out, has served as chaplain for the Dallas Mavericks basketball and the Dallas Cowboys football teams, and has been honored by the Family Research Council in recognition of his dedication to protecting, encouraging, and strengthening the American family.)

ORGANIZATIONS FIGHTING FOR BETTER EDUCATION IN AMERICA:

Center for Parent Youth Understanding (CPYU)
President: Walt Mueller
P.O. Box 414
Elizabethtown, PA 17022
(717) 361-8429
Website: www.cpyu.org
(Dedicated to educating and updating parents, teachers, and youth workers on current trends in a rapidly changing youth culture. Will work with churches, schools, and community organizations to build strong families based upon the Gospel of Jesus Christ.)

<u>Christian Schools International</u> (CSI)
3350 East Paris Avenue S.E.
Grand Rapids, MI 49512-3054
(616) 957-1070
Website: www.gospelcom.net/csi/
(A private, nonprofit organization founded in 1920, CSI is a community of Christian day
schools and affiliated institutions which share a Reformed, Christian perspective. CSI's
mission is to advance Christian education and to support schools in their task of teaching
students to know God and to glorify him through obedient service.)

<u>Citizen's for Excellence in Education</u> (CEE)
President: Robert L. Simonds
P.O. Box 3200
Costa Mesa, CA 92628
(714) 251-9333
Website: www.nace-cee.org
Radio: *Issues in Education*
Newsletter: *Family Building Blocks*
(A division of the National Association of Christian Educators, CEE helps Christian
parents and teachers to replace faith-destroying curricula with programs that support
traditional moral values and restore a safe public school environment which provides
academic excellence. CEE can help you organize parents in your district to form a local
CEE chapter—your most effective way to have input to your local school board.)

<u>Educational Research Analysts</u>
Founders: Mel and Norma Gabler
P.O. Box 7518
Longview, TX 75607-7518
(903) 753-5993
Website: http://members.aol.com/txbkrevws/
(Review public school textbooks for historical accuracy.)

ORGANIZATIONS FIGHTING AGAINST THE TEACHING OF EVOLUTIONARY
THEORY AS FACT:

<u>Answers in Genesis</u>
Executive Director: Ken Ham
Authoritative Speaker: Dr. Gary Parker
P.O. Box 6330
Florence, KY 41022
(606) 727-2222
Website: www.AnswersInGenesis.org
Newsletter: *Answers*
(Ministry centers on the teaching of Biblical foundations and the origin of man. At their
seminars, workshops, and museum settings, they provide easy-to-understand answers to
difficult questions about creation and the book of Genesis in particular.

<u>Institute for Creation Research</u> (ICR)
President Emeritus: Henry Morris
President: John D. Morris, Ph.D.
10946 Woodside Ave. N., Santee, CA 92071

P.O. Box 2667, El Cajon, CA 92021
(619) 448-0900
Website: www.icr.org
Radio: *Science, Scripture, and Salvation* and *Back to Genesis.*
Newsletter: *Acts & Facts*
(Founded by Henry M. Morris, ICR has a full-time science staff of eight Ph.D.'s and one
Ed.D., as well as seventeen fully accredited teachers, researchers, and speakers who
comprise their adjunct/visiting staff. ICR spearheads Biblical Christianity's defense
against the godless dogma of evolutionary humanism that has dominated our educational
system. They hold seminars, debates, and tours, and provide science programs, a
graduate school, books, tapes, videos, and a daily devotional Bible-study booklet which is
published quarterly entitled "Days of Praise.")

LEGAL ORGANIZATIONS:

<u>Alliance Defense Fund</u>
President: Alan Sears
7819 East Greenway Road, Suite 8
Scottsdale, AZ 85260
(888) 233-9990 or (800) TELL ADF
E-mail: aesadf@azlink.com

<u>American Center For Law and Justice</u> (ACLJ)
President: Pat Robertson
Chief Counsel: Jay Sekulow
P.O. Box 64429
Virginia Beach, VA 23467
(757) 579-2489
Website: www.aclj.org
(A not-for-profit public interest law firm and educational organization comprised of a
network of attorneys who are committed to the defense of Judeo-Christian values and
dedicated to the promotion of pro-liberty, pro-life and pro-family causes. Provides legal
services, renders advice and council to clients, and supports attorneys who are involved
in defending the religious and civil liberties of Americans.)

<u>Home School Legal Defense Association</u>
President: Michael P. Farris
P.O. Box 3000
Purcellville, VA 20134
(540) 338-5600
Website: www.hslda.org
Radio: *Home School Heartbeat*
Newsletter: *Home School Court Report*
(Founded in 1983, this organization is committed to home education not only as a legal
right, but also as an educational opportunity and spiritual blessing. They defend and
advance the constitutional rights of parents to direct the education of their children while
providing low-cost, yet quality legal defense for home schooling families through means
of networking.)

<u>Liberty Council</u>
Founder: Atty. Mathew Staver

P.O. Box 540774
Orlando, FL 32854-1776
(404) 875-2100
(Non-profit legal organization dedicated to defending religious liberties.)

The National Legal Foundation (NLF)
President: Steven W. Fitschen
P.O. Box D
Chesapeake, VA 23328
(757) 424-4242
Website: www.nlf.net
Newsletter: *Minuteman*
(A public interest law firm founded in 1985 that is dedicated to the preservation of
America's freedom and constitutional rights. This organization seeks to protect
America's legal system from being usurped to ends which run counter to God's purposes,
pursue legal and policy means of ensuring that all levels of government reward good and
punish evil, train Christian scholars, statesmen, lawyers, and jurists who will positively
impact the nation, and educate the American people regarding legal and public policy
issues. NLF is committed to providing free legal assistance to any community that wants
to enact an Issue 3 type ordinance—a city charter amendment that would prohibit the
granting of special rights to gays.)

The Rutherford Institute
President: John Whitehead
1445 East Rio Road
P.O. Box 7482
Charlottesville, VA 22906
(804) 978-3888
Website: www.rutherford.org
Radio: *Freedom Under Fire*
National Weekly Newspaper Column: *Freedom Under Fire*
Newsletter: *Action*
(A nonprofit, civil liberties organization with a network of over 2,300 affiliate attorneys
that are dedicated to preserving free speech in the public arena, including public schools,
defending religious freedom in the workplace, protecting the rights of churches, church
schools, home schools, and other religious organizations to operate freely without
improper state intrusion, safeguarding parental and family rights from government
intrusion, supporting the sanctity of human life, and defending individuals who are
being persecuted for their faith. Provides a "Religious Liberty" bulletin, books, audio
and videotapes, pamphlets, booklets and a home schooler series.)